ELUSIVE EQUITY, EMPATHY, *and* EMPOWERMENT

ELUSIVE EQUITY, EMPATHY, *and* EMPOWERMENT

One Woman's Journey through the Challenges of Gender Bias in the Early Twenty–First Century

Empowerment

Shared Decision Making

Fairness - Equity

Tolerance - Empathy

Amplify All Contributions

Inclusion - Teamwork

Listen to All Voices - Respect

Pandora B. Angel, MD

ARCHWAY
PUBLISHING

Archway Publishing books may be ordered through booksellers or by contacting:

Archway Publishing
1663 Liberty Drive
Bloomington, IN 47403
www.archwaypublishing.com
1 (888) 242-5904

Title Page Image Credit: Pandora B. Angel, MD
Interior Image Credits: Pandora B. Angel, MD
Domestic Abuse Intervention Programs

ISBN: 978-1-4808-6826-7 (sc)
ISBN: 978-1-4808-6825-0 (hc)
ISBN: 978-1-4808-6827-4 (e)

Library of Congress Control Number: 2018911481

Print information available on the last page.

Archway Publishing rev. date: 10/4/2018

To my parents, my children, and my husband.

On Elusive Equity

Women dream of equitable careers in all professions. Women should be empowered to use their skill sets and talents to the fullest.

"Our industry must recognize that women who dream of careers in music face barriers that men have never faced. We must actively work to eliminate these barriers and encourage women to live their dreams and express their passion and creativity through music." (Grammy Chief Neil Portnow, 1-30-18)

On the Golden Rule

"Once there was a gentile who came before <u>Shammai</u>, and said to him: 'Convert me on the condition that you teach me the whole Torah while I stand on one foot. Shammai pushed him aside with the measuring stick he was holding. The same fellow came before Hillel, and Hillel converted him, saying: That which is despicable to you, do not do to your fellow, this is the whole <u>Torah</u>, and the rest is commentary, go and learn it.'" (Babylonian Talmud)

Contents

Introduction

My name is Pandora Angel. I have been a practicing physician for thirty years. During those years, I spent twenty-three years as an emergency physician at a university medical center and an affiliated hospital. This book is not about the well-documented drama of emergency medicine, but about the challenges I faced as a female emergency physician in what is still perceived as a male profession. Although half of medical school graduating classes are made up of women (Contorno 2014), the decision-making bodies are still very much male dominated. I wrote this book to add the voice of a female physician. Women as a group confront additional hurdles throughout their personal and professional lives that may be unbeknownst to male colleagues. As individual incidents, many demeaning and undermining events appear seemingly insignificant or a mere slight. But over a lifespan, the additional toll and energy drain for women struggling to excel and succeed is monumental. It requires a lot of effort to overcome the negative aspects of our culture toward women to have good lives as working women and mothers.

This is a partial memoir about the gender bias and inequality I experienced while striving for and achieving a career in medicine. Many gratifying and fulfilling experiences throughout my life are withheld from this memoir to stay on point and not self-embellish my great privilege and fortune as an upper-middle-class American citizen. There are no mentions of chocolate, clogs, airplane adventures, beloved pets, childhood and parenting milestones, NFL football, or NCAA basketball. This is not a complete autobiography. The early chapters provide the social context and backdrop for the latter chapters, which address workforce power and control, double standards, gender bias, discrimination, the boys' club, harassment, contrived narratives for predetermined goals, retaliation, disregard for objective data, and misconceptions.

This book is not centered on patient care or the sensationalized career of a female emergency physician. This book is focused on a persistent culture of inequity in the workplace from my perspective as a female physician in a male-dominated field. This thoughtful exploration of vignettes, lessons, and appendices might be instructive for large companies and academic institutions that may falsely believe inequity is being adequately addressed today (Cauterucci 2016). The appendices highlight the need for hope and inspiration to act in this moment of time, the commonality of workplace bias and inequality, the fundamentals of good workplace processes, effective feedback basics, error recognition, harassment education, a suggested reading list, and community resources. Two pyramids, one on conflict and one on action, visually summarize the overarching concepts that crush or empower individuals in society in general and the workforce in particular. These pyramids provide a framework for future discussions on dysfunctional or effective relationships.

The vignettes drawn from my experiences as a female physician will be recognizable to some degree by most women in any workplace. From the backdrop of my experiences, I will delve into the more general nature of gender bias with thoughtful and philosophical discussions. Teaching tools and lessons will be provided at the end of each chapter in the hope to stimulate wider discussions of inequality, harassment, bias, and discrimination that still occur. Some illustrations are quite negative but are balanced by the hope that individual and community action will lead to change and progress for all individuals in the workplace. Our personal and professional lives can be even more satisfying and rewarding.

Read and believe. This partial memoir describes a childhood dream, gender issues and struggles to achieve and maintain this dream, and a premature end to this dream due to gender issues and perceived implicit bias. In our current culture, men who reach out to others often find new opportunities. Although women may replicate some male behaviors, the identical actions for women may lead to opportunities but are also likely to lead to potential victimization. Mentor relationships offered by individuals like Bill Cosby are just one example.

This writing is a potential awareness raising for those who wish to further understand the quagmire many still experience in self-expression, mutual respect, and understanding in the workforce. Both men and women in the workforce will benefit from a greater understanding of gender bias and unconscious bias of all nature affecting the livelihood of many individuals. This book is one story about a search for equity, empathy, and empowerment. I believe most men in the workforce behave appropriately. Some men are inappropriate due to blind spots and hidden biases (Banaji 2013). Some men are less capable than their female counterparts. Unfortunately, men and some women appear to have more job security and potential career advancement by supporting the male tribe/team rather than ethically holding inappropriate men accountable and supporting female colleagues in their struggles for equality.

It has been my good fortune to have a full life with a family and a career. I perceive myself to be a grandmother, mother, daughter, and spouse in a blended, ecumenical family. I am a physician, teacher, researcher, activist, advocate, friend, and colleague. I have been known to transform any bad event into a fun outing; the glass is always half-full. My belief in the goodness and best intentions of most individuals is strong. My work and passion have been an advocacy for underrepresented individuals and survivors of violence. I broadened into communication styles and empathy as a natural extension of work with colleagues with whom I had shared other common projects. Choosing to work as a physician is choosing to live in service to others with truth and integrity. This truth, at times, would prove to be inconvenient.

"Everything can be taken from a man but one thing: the last of human freedoms—to choose one's attitude in any given set of circumstances, to choose one's own way." (Viktor Frank, *Man's Search for Meaning*)

"We must always take sides. Neutrality helps the oppressor, never the victim. Silence encourages the tormentor, never the tormented." (Elie Wiesel, *The Night Trilogy: Night, Dawn, the Accident*)

"Speaking truth to power means believing deeply in what you say and fighting every day to have that heard. It may not be popular; it means taking a risk, it means standing for something." (Bayard Rustin, civil rights leader)

My life to date seems to be based in three realms: family, faith, and medicine. My childhood family included loving parents and three siblings. My subsequent blended family includes a loving spouse and six children, three by birth and three by marriage; this is our version of *The Brady Bunch*. We currently have six grandchildren. My father exemplified a strong work ethic and exuded aspirations for his children. My mother was an excellent listener; she reminded me at intervals of the unfairness of life circumstances. This lesson freed me to strive for justice and fairness while not taking misrepresentations and false narratives too much to heart. Good listeners surrounding me assisted with the pain of life and prompted me to work on my listening skills. My daughters remind me I still have much work to do. Even as a non-helicopter parent, the instinct to smooth the journey for children, and those following behind, is strong. I am the individual who is unable to go to horror movies and will spontaneously shout out protective suggestions like "Don't open that door!" in adventure PG-13 movies.

Medicine, as a career and lifestyle, has allowed me to practice empathy: "I am sorry." This career path also uncovered the biases (conscious or unconscious) that persist in our large institutions. Change comes far too slowly for the activist, change-the-world personality with which I was born. Leadership qualities, energy, and determination are assets until you hit the glass ceiling of the current, entrenched nature of large institutions. Sometimes it takes only a few individuals, possibly with unconscious biases, to stop you in your tracks. The medical profession is supposed to be about caring and "first do no harm" as recited in the Hippocratic Oath. However, maladaptive behaviors to obtain and retain power and control in large institutions, as in society, are universal.

The unfortunate reminder that I am not one of the guys reared its head routinely but did not blunt my interest in moving forward. Learning about empathy and empowerment were helpful to me as a clinician and a person. The triple threat of juggling academic medicine includes clinical, research, and teaching responsibilities. The triple support of life includes faith, family, and friends. These challenges and support systems brought me through a lifetime of advocacy and have empowered me to write this book of my experiences and perceptions as a platform to influence views on equality for women.

My goals have been to live my values, strive to understand life's perceptions and misperceptions, and attempt to make life fun. I value integrity and truth. Communication is important to allow individuals to represent themselves as they choose to be perceived. Perception may be a gift and a curse. I have been able to perceive many circumstantial disconnects, motivations, and threats to avert potential disasters. The Cassandra syndrome—seeing disaster but being unable to avert it— might be invoked on occasion in my lifetime. I have also been able to recognize patterns, possibly through delayed intuition, to allow more efficient analyses and problem solving.

My lessons and teachings seem to surround equity, empathy, and empowerment. Fairness was identified as relevant early in life as an identical twin. Empathy has been pivotal as a family member and physician. Empowerment to move myself, others, and the world community forward is evolution. This mixture of life stories, both personal and professional, represent the identity and struggle for balance experienced by most women in the workforce. Many situations are addressed differently today, showing signs of progress. Whereas other scenarios resound seemingly little changed after decades of discussion.

Many injustices and immoralities are simply awful but lawful. Culture change is needed. Bad behavior in academia persists because it can without accountability. Individuals who attempt to improve the work environment with raised awareness are often retaliated against and/or removed from the environment for divisive behavior. Patterns of behavior often demonstrate a disregard for the welfare of women. Women are responding, "Time's up." The storytelling and subsequent analyses are evidence that sexual harassment is merely the tip of the iceberg of inequity in the workplace (see Conflict Pyramid, page 94). Women want diverse, moral leadership and decision-making bodies. Systemic abuse of power is not acceptable.

History shows spurts of societal action and change. We are in such a moment today. We recall the former separation of the workforce and the home environment primarily by gender. Women started to work outside the home in the late nineteenth and early twentieth centuries. We may reflect on the prior limitation of women to select careers, including secretary, teacher, child care provider, and nurse. Women were often helpers in the male power structure of the workforce. We acknowledge the women's movement of the 1970s with protests for change. Only at this time did women appear in any recognizable numbers in the male-dominated professions. Some career tracks are approaching parity in the workforce today, but other professions lag miserably behind and hold tightly to gender-based ideologies and processes.

The years 2017 and 2018 have been a powerful watershed for addressing sexual harassment in the workplace. More universally, gender bias is experienced by women in the workplace with career-limiting and even career-ending implications. Society can no longer normalize or justify through ignorance clear gender bias and discrimination that exists in the workplace. The year 2017 was a surge forward for empowerment and a devastating recognition of pervasive victimization. This book is one woman's thoughtful exploration on this time period to maintain momentum for justice for all. It is a call to action. As a whole society, we must have the courage to confront adverse situations resulting from bias. The stories illustrated can occur in all workplaces and will provide a basis from which readers can decide to react if confronted with similar situations in their particular work environment.

> "It was the best of times, it was the worst of times, it was the age of wisdom, it was the age of foolishness, it was the epoch of belief, it was the epoch of incredulity, twas the season of light, it was the season of darkness, it was the spring of hope, it was the winter of despair."
> (Charles Dickens, *A Tale of Two Cities*)

All lives have success and failure. I am no different; I see myself as every woman, only one of womankind. But let it be clear: women are not failing. Institutions and administrations are failing to fairly incorporate women. The time is up for silence. I choose to stand in my truth, embrace the positive, and learn from the negative. I did not simply persevere despite adversity—I thrived. My writing comes from a place of passion in a consequential year for myself and women. People who have been victimized with violence, social injustice, gender bias, economic discrimination can be resilient (Kahlo 2013), effective, and even skillful with informative experiences. Survivors are not less credible or less than. Survivors can be assets, problem solvers, and agents of change. I chose to think globally but act locally.

Often perpetrators believe victims will not tell their stories out of fear of retaliation, victim blaming, and embarrassment. I tell many stories. Maybe my experiences are more numerous than others, but society will never know the extent of the Me Too movement if individuals are not willing to start sharing. One-third of women have experienced discrimination in the workplace (Covert 2013). Victimization is a failure not of the victim but of the institutions that do not hold the perpetrators accountable. The courage to be vulnerable changes the way people live (Brown 2012). There is cultural overlap between societal and work environments. Awareness of victimization can lead to empowerment.

Likewise, awareness of harassment, gender bias, and discrimination may lead to future equality through policy change.

Similarity exists in an episode for United States Ambassador to the United Nations Nikki Haley in 2018 following a United Nations statement about Russia sanctions. She was not kept in the loop as decisions changed. She was described as having "momentary confusion" and then being "in a box" by Larry Kudlow, a White House economic adviser. President Trump doesn't appear to like strong people around him and feels threatened. Public suggestions of a possible Pence-Haley ticket for 2020 election hangs in the air. Ambassador Haley, who is recognized as consistently responsible and prepared, retorted, "With all due respect, I don't get confused" (*The Guardian* April 17, 2018).

My intent is not to identify or blame any individuals but to address a broad cultural and institutional inequity that still exists. I do not want to sound like sour grapes or respond to inevitable victim blaming that may ensue. The believability that an exemplary student and employee until the age of fifty suddenly becomes a problem in a work setting is simply not credible. This is a reconstruction exercise to address confirmation bias and improve understanding of persistent gender bias. This exercise may guide other employees with their future interactions.

Some may be happy with the status quo. Some may actually defend and normalize the status quo. I experienced a lifetime of gender disparity. Susan B. Anthony would remind us that failure is impossible. Have hope. Individual and group action is the only path forward to address societal biases.

> "Never give up. Never become bitter. Be hopeful. Be optimistic and Keep pushing." (John Lewis, January 16, 2017)

> "One of the things I think about this book (*Fire and Fury*) and why it's hit such a chord and become this cultural moment is it's given everybody this focused opportunity to say 'holy crap.'" (Michael Wolff, author of *Fire and Fury*, January 7, 2018)

Prologue

Finally the day arrived. The meeting had been rescheduled by hospital administrators, maybe more than once. This meeting was placed on my calendar as a general discussion. The purpose of the meeting was to discuss interdepartmental issues that had been ignored for years. The administrative team had avoided transparency, open discussions, meetings, and even e-mails.

My excitement rose for the opportunity to discuss communication and operational issues that could improve patient care and staff satisfaction. As an accomplished emergency physician of twenty-seven years, I had prepared. I spent time outlining ideas. I walked on my college campus with a former classmate discussing this upcoming meeting and pondering nonviolence and conflict resolution exuded by those of us who lived at Peace House during college. We visited the grave site of our university church pastor and philosophy professor. I remembered the activism, including conscientious objector status pamphlets handed out at the post office. I had collected articles including "Sandberg: Women are Leaning In-but Face Pushback" and books including Sheryl Sandberg's 2013 *Lean In* that explained what I and so many others had experienced in the workforce and life. I had suggested this reading to male leadership. I was well versed in communication styles and feedback for operational change.

As per my routine, I arrived early. I arranged the chairs in the room and cleaned off scattered items from prior gatherings. I poised myself at the head of the table, or maybe the foot of the table; I had never been invited to prior meetings to see the typical seating arrangement. My folder of notes and displays was placed squarely on the table. I practiced some lines and watched the clock. I reminded myself to keep a steady voice, never shrill or abrasive (Kieran 2014). Women conform to speaking in controlled fashions to avoid negative stereotypes (Streitfeld 2015). Try to be agreeable but do not concede the facts that are undeniable. Five minutes after the hour, no one else had arrived. I texted my husband to laugh and subdue some rising anticipation of the interactions to come.

Two administrators arrived. I opened the meeting and bantered lightly about the NPR show with medical implications I had heard driving into work solely for this meeting. I had no office currently; I worked from home when not assigned to clinical shifts. When the third administrator appeared and only one additional administrator was absent, I began some introductory remarks. I transitioned to a patient complaint article that I had in hand that described complaints as an opportunity to improve interactions as the fourth and final administrator arrived. The discussion progressed into a general discussion of the interdepartmental patient hand-off issue; this entailed the transfer of pertinent information for continuity of patient care.

After concerns were aired, I respectfully broached the theory of relativity (common knowledge of physics for most physicians) and views from different perspectives. I shared my routine experience of receiving short, one-line comments by the overnight team prior to my day shift. The hospital administrator became immediately defensive and stated the night staff were clearly busy. He further stated the day staff expected any and all necessary information to be provided verbally upon request rather than reviewed in the electronic record. I had no intention of chastising anyone but merely showed the great disparity of expectations and responses between two services on opposite sides of a hand-off. I explicitly stated I was not angry with anyone but was seeking a better process. I made a positive comment about an emergency physician who utilized the electronic record hand-off and noted the inconsistent use of any formal hand-off in the observation unit to provide further variations.

Once these variabilities were aired, I looked at a senior administrator and stated that I'd previously met with the chair of the emergency department at the university hospital biannually for fifteen years. This female chair said when presented with similar communication mishaps, "People complain. Keep up the great work." Complaints happened in the work setting.

The administrator who'd arrived late, as per his custom, interrupted. Seated across from the senior administrator, he burst out of his chair, yelled, "I don't have to take this," and stormed out of the room. He returned within less than a minute to yell at me, "You can leave this job if you don't like it," or something close to that.

A second administrator, a friend of the first who'd departed the meeting, exited the room to comfort this individual. He returned to instruct me, "You need to apologize." In the *Huffington Post*, Gray draws attention to our culture that makes women apologize constantly. Hillary Clinton was the first presidential candidate to apologize in a concession speech (Wieczner 2016; Gray 2015).

The hospital administrator asked, "Why are you always a problem?" and exited. The senior administrator appeared uncomfortable and attempted to leave the room. I stated I needed to speak with him. I revealed that the distraught administrator was a non-communicator and was the cause of numerous staff departures and misunderstandings; he appeared insecure and threatened by my skill set and staff support within our unit. Staff retention and consistent unit performance was a concern. I too had been scouting out alternate career opportunities for the past couple years. I perceived each male administrator in this meeting as clinging to his tribal comfort zone and shunning me as a female outsider. No one appeared interested in situational awareness or conflict resolution. Male talking points and narratives were already engrained. I was informed I needed to "do my part." This senior administrator requested names of individuals with whom he would speak, continuing the misguided paper trails and escalating animosity toward me. This reprimand of individuals oversimplifies and betrays the goal of changing a misogynistic culture. I offered no names. The administrator inserted the names of the usual suspects. Thus ended the meeting in little more than thirty minutes, including the late arrival of several participants.

Astonishment overwhelmed me. This male medical administrator would not hold meetings with me despite our common clinical practice setting and he discouraged e-mail dialogue or any written documentation about process issues. He met only for the purpose of informing me of spurious operational complaints for a paper trail. He had succeeded in prematurely ending the general discussion in anger to control the narrative. Consensus and team building were not his apparent goals for this meeting. He created agitation and provocation to distract and muddy reality. He manufactured a narrative of a poor-fitting employee—me. It was my rare opportunity to air my previously unheard perspectives after years of being silenced, isolated, and misrepresented.

A follow-up e-mail discussed my perspective, which had been denied in the truncated meeting. It was simply not credible that I was either unaware of my situation or unable to articulate this predicament to the administrative hierarchy.

> 10-12-16
>
> Dear _____,
>
> Thank you for the opportunity to dialogue with you today.
>
> It is always difficult when issues are larger than initially framed. But hearing maladaptive behaviors for years without adequate resolution is a reality in the workforce. I have attempted to address issues with ___ in writing because he prefers no meetings. I have approached ____ in writing and in person, to which he appears more amenable lately. I have written individual hospitalists and ____ with little to no response but some change in behavior.
>
> All I request is that I am respected and allowed to have a voice in the unit, department, and hospital

at which I intend to dedicate the next ten years of my career. I am highly respected and appreciated by the staff I interact with on a daily basis. I provide excellent care as I have during my entire career.

The difficulties arise when I am disrespected and distrusted due to inaccurate innuendo and lack of administrative support to the individuals who are frustrated. I have always performed above the standard, and at this more advanced stage of my career, I am willing to speak out about the inequities that exist in the workforce. No male attending with thirty years of clinical experience would be treated like a subordinate by youthful attending physicians on another service.

I am pleased that ED and EOU administration speak well of me in public settings in your presence, but I must reiterate that the communication in the EOU is all but absent and solely negative until recently. Efforts to encourage my resignation and collect negative narratives are blatantly obvious to me and will not be tolerated. I have no faith that ___will accurately comprehend or convey perspectives foreign to him. He has great insecurity due to staffing lapses and performance metrics.

___'s late arrival to our meeting and abrupt departure are immature and unprofessional when we are working on team building. His inability to respond in a professional manner in this meeting was the event that turned the meeting—not my initial statement that informed the group that administrative de-escalation is required when staff members lower themselves to in-fighting. Methinks he doth protest too much. This comment was directed to a group of administrators, all of whom have had an opportunity to deescalate inter-department matters.

I appreciate finally dialoguing with an individual who can listen and see many perspectives to every interaction. Thank you. I am looking forward to years of future interactions to improve patient care at this hospital.

Pandora

My usual schedule for the next two months continued. Interactions with off-service providers actually improved. I smiled knowing that difficult discussions sometimes need to happen to create the understanding and inertia for change. I felt badly at one routine department meeting where one administrator appeared more despondent; he could not make eye contact. No further interaction occurred between me and these four administrators. Clearly taking issues to a group forum where ideas and perspectives were openly aired could point out blind spots and unconscious bias in individual administrative assessments. However, the priority must be patient care and consistent, efficient processes, especially in this changing world for health care and cost containment.

On a Tuesday, I was working clinically. It was a busy day, but in usual style, patients were getting efficient, quality care. Staff were catching up on their documentation. I was reading my mail when a phone call came. A meeting was arranged for the end of my shift with two administrators. I was available and said I would be there. I knew the meaning. I sat for a moment reflecting, almost like that pre-death sensation of my life flashing before me. But this was my career. This had been my dream since age ten. This was my struggle for my entire education and training. This was my identity. This was my means for caring for my family. This was my contribution to changing the world and making it a better place.

My daze broke. I went into slow, methodical action. I cleaned out my one file drawer and inconspicuously took things to my car. I called one nurse into the hall. She continued with mindless chatter that previously was a relief from detail work between the ebbs and flow of patient care. I explained my suspected situation. She was stunned. I returned to the clinical setting and waited for shift change. I signed out to the physician assistant and again sought the privacy of the hallway to reveal my suspicions. He proclaimed spontaneously, "But you would be great for the new unit" currently finishing construction. I told him I would be okay in spite of this clear, high-suicide risk factor compounding a lifetime of stressors. I had a wonderful mother who explained, "Life is not fair." I was simply part of this life. The physician assistant had already given his notice to transfer to another department because the director in the unit was impossible to work with. He would be okay too. Both staff members aware of my situation requested feedback after the meeting.

I arrived at the meeting with an extended handshake to distancing leadership. These administrators told me that my services were no longer required at the university, and my appointment would not be renewed. I was provided a letter of nonrenewal of my faculty appointment. I believe this action was pre-orchestrated for an extensive period of time. I had prepared for such an event and provided no drama for these two younger, male physicians I had trained. After inquiring about whether I was excused, I left the room with no fanfare.

This pronouncement was the professional equivalent of Trump's infamous "You're Fired," without the implication of clinical incompetence. The reality exists: an institution can always remove a staff member if it chooses. Administrators can always put some negative narrative in a file, even if contrived. The bot attacks remind us of the power of controlling any narrative. At issue is whether any given, inaccurate narrative is immoral or illegal.

The text to my two confidants was sent: "It is so." I was thankful for all the well-wishes in e-mails, texts, and cards that I received. I felt connected and appreciated by so many, but by not the people who made the decisions. I would not have suspected that a physician with my career track could be derailed by rare, incidental operational issues with misrepresentation into a negative narrative by less experienced and lower-performing individuals. I did not seek their positions.

Nonetheless, there was obviously a tension, an opposition to sharing any power, control, or decision making with me, and these individuals could not endure it. Of note, one administrator wrote an e-mail to the entire emergency staff sent later that day, stating I had been "an integral part of our unit from the very start. Her dedication to the care of our patients has been greatly appreciated." Irony and hypocrisy drip from this statement.

I drove home planning to call my attorney the next day. She would console me that I had at least survived six years since a contentious contract dispute—not bad. We had successfully negotiated a new contract to my satisfaction after a department restructuring. I was not tearful. I had seen the target on my back and the writing on the wall for at least five years. I was actually relieved to be released from the maladaptive environment. Carrying the torch for the cause of morality and equality was exhausting. Living up to higher standards demanded an eventual verdict. I felt like collateral damage for necessary institutional change. I would miss the patients and my friends. I would enjoy my family and more free time. I had prepared for this eventuality.

University legal counsel would eventually attribute this disrupted meeting to an "unwarranted attack" by me on male leadership. This is quite a spin on an attempt at civil discourse for process improvement. This assessment felt like micro-aggression to me. Words matter. Cognitive transfer and confirmation bias over years with an unopposed negative narrative against me, promulgated by a few male leaders (some with limited administrative and communication skills), were insurmountable. My voice would never be heard in a meeting. Christine Lagarde, a French lawyer and the managing director of the International Monetary Fund, called out men at a world economic forum, revealing, "When the woman starts talking, the men switch off" (Parker 2017). This behavior does not appear to be the case with all men, just some. This habit of some men may be culturally learned in the home or work environment. Of note, one hospital administrator was no longer in his administrative role within a year of my completed employment. However, he was still employed and I was not. Broad-reaching education on hand-off procedures was also implemented.

Reflection is inevitable. So many interpersonal encounters. So many events. So many lessons. So much more change necessary to approach equity in the world. I gained so much from the insights of those before me and wondered what I might have to share.

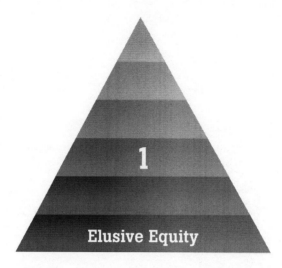

1

Elusive Equity

My childhood revolved around a family home, school, and church. Faith was central to our family, which attended church routinely on Sundays and participated in choirs, youth groups, committees, and church retreats. Family values also included my grandmother's mantra of moderation with Methodist tones, as well as efforts to simply do one's best because that was all one was gifted to do. Faith also carried us through life's events. Remembering one is not alone while believing in something greater than oneself is reassuring and humbling. Everyone is a survivor of some nature. Caring for others and an early sense of advocacy formulated my framework of life. My grandmother witnessed the 1920 ratification of the nineteenth amendment and never missed an election for which she was eligible to vote.

In the beginning, I was born prematurely. I was the first of a pair of identical twins, each weighing less than four pounds in an era before pediatric intensive care units. I learned years later that this was a difficult day for my mother. She was informed by the pediatrician that she should avoid seeing her newborn daughters because we were not expected to survive. Perinatal grief management has since evolved (Badenhorst 2007; Forrest 1982). She nonetheless visited us daily for weeks in the hospital until we were released to join our older brother and parents in a studio apartment of the University Park apartments.

These apartments are better known to locals as "white pants ghetto" for the hospital attire of training physicians. My entry into the world was stamped with, "You are a survivor."

As a medical student, during my pediatric rotation in the new-born nursery, I heard my former childhood pediatrician rounding on patients, and I introduced myself. He gave me an overwhelming bear hug. I realized that this man had invested a great deal in my health and well-being. I recalled only well child checks. My mother was reassured that her daughters were healthy but simply not on the growth curve of all the other children our age. I was on my own path of life.

Further in my career, as a young attending physician, a colleague who had visited multiple cities and institutions in his training repeat-edly inquired about my protracted time in the same community in a needling fashion, as if it was a detriment to my career. I usually lis-tened politely and assured him I had traveled to numerous locations for conferences and pleasure. One day as this line of inquiry continued, I threw down the gauntlet and blurted out, "I was born in this hospital." The topic was never entertained again. I valued my family and home community. I saw no reason why I could not simultaneously cherish my family, faith, and career.

My childhood was filled with the fun of playing cards, in particular solitaire, bridge and gin. My mother grew up in a strict Methodist house-hold where this activity had been prohibited. I grew to love numbers, including totaling restaurant receipts and playing Yahtzee. Words were equally fun with Scrabble and Agatha Christie novels. Life was full of wonder and goodness. I had little idea about the tumult of the 1960s except for seeing my mother cry while President Lyndon B. Johnson announced the death of President John F. Kennedy. I recalled one babysit-ter with inappropriate fondling, which confused me and mortified my mother when I told her as an adult. She exclaimed that she thought this sitter was well liked by her children. The sitter took us into town for do-nuts. I could only agree with her assessment. Grooming works by mixing positive behaviors with elements of abuse (Samsel 2008). The confusion of interpersonal abuse and victimization would weave into my career.

Needless to say, while growing up as an identical twin, fairness and equity are important qualities (Free Library 2010). Everything was in fact identical for years. As choices could be made, everything was similar but a different color. Comparisons and self-assessments were a normal part of every aspect of daily life. However, in my search for fairness, I did notice early in my childhood that the boys received different treatment. Acquaintances repeatedly asked me if I would become a nurse, never considering a physician. This intended encouragement followed gender standards for medicine but was not truly the steps of my physician father. I performed well in math even though the clear assumption was that boys would succeed at a higher level in this subject area.

At a young age, I became a girl with a mission. I wanted to be a physician. I derived true pleasure and a sense of fun from problem solving. I felt terribly confused when a boy in second grade skipped third grade and I did not. I knew he had a perfect score on the math quizzes completed weekly during the entire year, but I had only missed one answer. I felt equally baffled when a boy in third grade received a scholarship to a private school in the area. I would treat a family member of this classmate late in my career. I extended greetings to this childhood friend, who was now working productively in a District of Columbia position. Only as an adult would I be told by my mother that each of these opportunities—skipping second grade and a private school scholarship—were declined by my parents in an effort to keep their twin daughters in the same grade and school. I would carry with me the realization that all decisions are multifactorial and have consequences.

My first male teacher was in fourth grade. It was awkward to play "around the world" with math facts. Students competed one-on-one. The student with the first correct response advanced to the next student and proceeded around the room. I stood when my turn arose and continued the process around the room until the teacher moved on to another activity. The teacher could no more instruct me to perform at a lower level than my ability allowed than a future colleague could tell me to see fewer patients or slow down. My brain didn't function that way; it was similar to a race car engine that performed better at a higher speed. The game didn't work with me participating. I aspired to be generous like my sixth grade teacher, who spoke with me as a friend and not down to me as a child. He provided more respect and autonomy to me than several adult colleagues in my future career as a physician. Where is Aretha Franklin, the queen of soul, to ask for a little respect for me?

Holding on to my joy of mathematics became a true scheduling issue in my college years. My advisor told me I needed only calculus, which I had completed in high school and partially repeated in college. Easing the scheduling of pre-medical requirements might push mathematics out of my schedule. I struggled with this idea and proceeded to declare a major in mathematics. Resilience and possibility were in my DNA. I could make it work out with a little thought and effort. Hurdles and stereotypes do impair women's careers in science (Reuben 2014).

> "So many women these days are striving for a new kind of American dream in STEM fields (Science, Technology, Engineering, and Math). But discouragingly, in a study of women in these fields, the *Atlantic* found women are literally being harassed out of science." (Williams 2016)

My inspirations in life were strong, empowering women like Susan B. Anthony, Eleanor Roosevelt, and Representative Louise Slaughter. My parents raised me to be independent and unconstrained by my gender. I spent considerable time in my elementary school years doing independent study, often in the hallway, to be able to concentrate on material beyond the class curriculum. This could have been misperceived as a disciplinary act by some staff if the school teachers had not made an effort to know me as an individual. Later in my career, completed tasks would be confused with inactivity rather than true efficiency and excellence. My high school math teacher was a brilliant woman and role model who was in a second career after working on the Manhattan Project. She was adored and inspired everyone. Later, as a young university community physician, I would see her in the emergency department visiting a patient. I approached her and had to exclaim, "I majored in math because of you." She smiled affectionately. Maintaining a connectedness to my upbringing, role models, and family was extremely helpful to my life journey.

The Methodist Church, along with my public school education, provided faith, values, and encouragement to achieve. Inclusion provided by the Methodist Church led to opportunities in music, fellowship, and mission outreach. To this day, I continue contact with several close friends from this fellowship. Several individuals are planning a reunion in the near future. Lessons of community, advocacy, teamwork, and inclusion were carried forward. As I ventured off to college, several church members mistook my pronouncement as an entrance into a divinity school in the community—a vocation still in the realm of possibility. Failure was impossible. Life was full of potential.

I avoided most personal criticisms and bullying in high school. However, I made a seemingly innocent comment to the grocer carrying a basket of fruit during a musical rehearsal of *Music Man*: "I'll squeeze your fruit." This comment received an unexpected piqued response as if telling a good joke, and so I reused the line. Cook-Garza describes the gender conundrum of humor in a 2015 book, *The Cool Girl Trap: Or Why Sexism in Tech Isn't Going Away*. Twelve years later, as an adult I became aware this comment was perceived with a negative sexual tone. Confusion without clarification may create misperceptions.

While seeking equality for girls, I learned about equality for all individuals. Anguish persisted over spontaneously laughing inappropriately when a boy's country of origin, Poland, was discussed in sixth grade social studies. I couldn't take it back. To date, I had only heard reference to this country in jokes. Later, as a young attending physician, I was grateful when a medical student gently told me a more appropriate term for future use when I spoke an outdated cultural term with no insult intended. I had used the term Oriental, not Asian. This was again a learned behavior from my Caucasian upbringing. Political and cultural correctness is a moving target. Diversity lessons come from sharing with each other. This honest and open communication helped make positive change in a potentially negative situation. Improvement toward tolerance and equality is the goal. Unfortunately, honest communication in the workplace is hard work. More universally, overwhelmed work environments often shun honest discussions. Essential features of mutual respect and trust for open dialogue are often lacking in intensely tribal work settings.

My natural ability was usually supplemented by a generous dose of luck or possibly what some might describe as divine intervention. Spiritual well-being has been associated with resilience (Smith 2013). In high school physics, multiple choice tests were the standard. After completing any given problem, the correct answer was the closest response that might in fact be many decimal points away from the true result. The physics teacher loved the confusion; the students, with no work shown, still had a 20 percent chance for a correct response on any question. Our first test was devastating to most. I had made an educated guess on four out of ten questions. Everyone wanted to know who'd broken the curve with a perfect score. I knew to say nothing. Girls in particular were not to brag or flaunt their higher achievement, especially if it outshined the boys.

Valuable time with my father included rounding at the hospital on Saturdays, in rotation with my siblings. On one occasion, I stood by a wall in the emergency department hallway to wait while my father examined a patient in a room. A flurry of activity and a procession of stretchers, police officers, and blood passed by. A nurse noted my wide-eyed expression and simply stated, "I don't think you were supposed to see that." Neither of us knew that I would spend thirty-one years treating patients in busy emergency departments. A childhood friend would be part of many memories with a great deal of freedom to wander the neighborhood. As an attending physician, I would care for her deceased father and inform the family of his death. Connectedness to the community, family, and friends continued during my medical career.

"But even if the culture of your workplace still oper-
ates with the traditional definition of success, you can
gather around you a group of like-minded people who
want to thrive and not just 'succeed.'" (Huffington,
Thrive)

The key lessons about equity in my youth would influence my future training and employment. Elusive equity continued. More lessons
would come.

Equity—Fairness

- The gender gap, implicit bias, and discrimination persist: positions,
  salaries, opportunities, mentors, recognition, acceptable behaviors, likeability, glass ceiling.
- Misogyny exists.
- Weaponization of information is used to control narratives.
- Women in power are portrayed more negatively.
- Strong, powerful women are often portrayed as annoying, prob-
  lematic, shunned, and dismissed, whereas powerful men are usually portrayed as assets and team members and are provided opportunities for retention and promotion.
- Loyalty to the boys' team and gender bias cannot supersede diversity, inclusion, objectivity, and fairness.

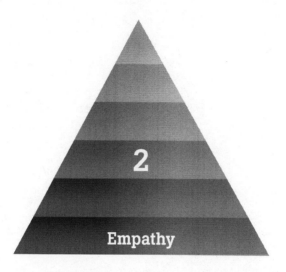

2

Empathy

My maturing and training years were filled with friends, college and medical school, and advocacy. I was involved in philanthropy with sorority life, Peace House, and church activities. Moving forward into these formidable years, my search for fairness transformed to empathy for those lacking just that fairness, the disadvantaged. Attending my college of choice was a good experience filled with academics, intramural sports, and opportunities to promote change. As a freshman, my father prompted me to live in the only solely female dormitory, part of a three-dorm complex. Unbeknownst to my parents, this dormitory complex was designed for single rooms on a single-gender (male) campus. The college celebrated ten years of female students on campus during my college years. Women comprised 50 percent of the United States college graduates in the early 1980s (Goldin 2006; Feeney 2015).

The halls of the now converted double rooms in a complex with a female, male, and mixed-gender structure were connected to each other by none other than the bathrooms, alternating bathroom gender on each floor. Students walking from one dorm to the next within this building complex knocked on the bathroom door and waited for five seconds, allowing any compromised person in the shower or at the sink to hit the wall or cover up before any number of individuals of the opposite sex passed through the bathroom as if it were Grand Central Station.

Beyond that unique feature, this freshman-only female dormitory was on the invite list for every fraternity party on campus for the whole year. Is anyone sensing potential vulnerability and victimization of a young, freshman population? In response, over the next several years a group of women (myself included) created the first sorority at this college. We selected the name Delta Nu to highlight change and, coincidentally, the thirteenth letter of the Greek alphabet. This local sorority went on to become a national sorority, Gamma Phi Beta, by the time I graduated in 1982. My daughters were quite surprised at their free spirit mother's Greek affiliation in college as they entered that time frame themselves. I explained that the Greek system was the only social structure. Women wanted to be empowered to organize social events, as well as community and educational activities.

My freshman year included a sorting phase in academics and socially. My college was known as a strong pre-medicine university. Of the twenty women on my floor, the vast majority were considering medicine as a potential career. Competition seeped over from the male students, one bathroom away. After the first semester, a few men, who were tracking GPA scores and ranking people and potential competitors, doggedly pursued me. I had already learned in junior high and high school to do my best but to not flaunt or reveal my test scores. I hear the Women's March of 2017: "Men of quality do not fear equality." Nonetheless, doing your best might be considered too much and lead to your demise if you outshine the boys and culturally shame them.

Tragedy struck our freshman class and dormitory when the competition and the transition phase from high school to college led to the suicide of one of our classmates (Fromme 2008). Heartache, empathy, and perspective were felt as a community. I continued into my subsequent semesters also aware that there was much less (and often no) subjectivity or potential bias to grades in the math and science courses. I could have more control over my own destiny. This would not be the case in future positions where others would control narratives. Unconscious bias appeared to exist in other subject areas. Some classmates were also victimized by predatory professors with unethical consensual relationships. This behavior still exists on university campuses due to lack of accountability. Unethical decision making often prioritizes staff retention, which is exacerbated in some geographical locations, especially if partners are also employed; reputation through enrollment numbers; and university revenue flow tracked with the endowment. This monetary prioritization may minimize the rights of individual people and morality. It may overshadow accountability for behavior (including criminal actions) inflicted on some staff and students. The code of silence persists.

During my sophomore and junior years, I lived at Ralph Bunche House, otherwise known as Peace House. Residents represented nonviolence, social activism, and diversity on campus. Ralph Bunche was an American political scientist, academic, and diplomat who received the 1950 Nobel Peace Prize for his mediation in Israel, the first African American to be so honored. There was a tea house in the basement for alternate social gatherings, as opposed to routine beer binges typical of the fraternity row. Every Monday evening, soup was served (usually lentil) to recognize global hunger. Many fellow students who were much more engaged in these issues and others, including apartheid, enlightened me. Several of these students later entered the Peace Corps and other service vocations. I had the privilege to be co-president with a great friend one year. Arranging speakers and events to balance our college experience was important to all the residents. Residents were preparing to have careers but also to be agents of change in the world.

One summer semester was required on campus. I had hoped to visit my twin sister before this summer semester on her campus. This would necessitate I take one final exam early. I succinctly requested this option with my reason and was denied. Days later, I tried a second one-line request and created anger in this professor. Incredulously, I tried a third time and blurted out, "I know I can't take the test on a different day. Might I just take it earlier in the day?" I succeeded, and the test took place, resulting in my lowest course grade for my college career, a B. I had a wonderful visit with my sister and her friends. I continued my summer semester in stride. Horrors of all horrors, what should I discover as I proceed into my junior year? This embryology professor was the chair of the premedical committee that wrote all letters of recommendation for medical school applicants. I believe the committee described me as a strong-willed woman who would reach her goals.

Finally, when I was a senior, six women joined together to rent a home that the landlord had previously only rented to men at this former all-male university. Housemates accentuated differences and reveled in attending different activities, particularly religious services of each housemate. We represented, as a group, atheism, Catholicism, Judaism, Protestantism, and the Religious Society of Friends, also known as Quakers. One housemate and I joined the Sojourners, a primarily African American gospel choir at the university church. We sought understanding through diversity. Professors were invited to dinner at our small kitchen table to discuss any issues of interest. Opportunities to grow as individuals were seized.

> "We should hope students will have learned how to find, evaluate and apply knowledge; how to work collaboratively; how to tolerate and manage uncertainty; how to reason; how to walk in someone else's shoes; how to relentlessly pursue what's best for each patient; how to debate, be wrong, fail—and embrace and learn from it, each time; how to become who they want to be." (Strauss 2017)

The professors at college also invited small groups of students to their homes for gatherings in this college town. One public speaking professor in particular had a beautiful home decorated for the winter holidays. He served eggnog with or without rum. I would retell stories of this delightful older professor only to discover my father had had this same professor for the same class. My father had found this class extremely helpful in his professional career, and I would discover the same conclusion. Other professors would expose us to their cultures and life lessons, including baklava and making time for relationships.

My father often had an operating room picnic at our home in my childhood years. This event included yard games and swimming. I carried on this generational tradition for several years and invited the emergency medicine residents to my home for their orientation gathering with faculty and staff. I offered this same social setting for the affiliated hospital observation unit, but this activity did not appear to fit into the plan for minimizing my role and marginalization. In and of itself, there would be no issue if a similar team-building event was offered elsewhere, but there was none. The male leadership even insinuated an undermining of his authority when unit women nurses (who kindly included me) decided to gather and decorate fingernails for fun. This assertion appeared to be a misguided projection of this leader's sense of vulnerability.

The math department had few women majoring in the subject area, despite no evidence across hundreds of studies that men in general have a statistically meaningful edge on women when it comes to math abilities (Lindberg 2010). We knew who we were. I ran under the radar as a premed student not majoring in the sciences. Many fellow students were completely bowled over when I declared my intention to go to medical school after college. My backup plans were teaching math or the ministry. I never counted my chickens before they hatched. I kept a low profile on my career goals. As a physician, I continued to hone in on a skill set of working quickly and accurately to get the correct answers. A college lucky number, thirteen, has stayed with me for life. I married on the thirteenth, I passed my medical boards on the thirteenth, my daughter was born on the thirteenth, my second daughter was born on the twenty-sixth, and my son (a bit late) was born on the fourteenth. Go figure! My fascination with numbers, combinations, and computations was second nature and fun.

When I applied for medical school, one interviewer inquired about whether I felt pressured to go into medicine with a parent in the field. I laughed and revealed my mother had cried when I told her my intentions. She had witnessed and shared my father's entire training and career. She was not interested in witnessing her daughter repeat these experiences. Nonetheless, as a caring parent, she supported me. Empathy from family members who support medical professionals and the lifestyle eases the stressors of daily life.

Not unexpectedly, medical school and residency training provided more challenges. Life balance became more elusive as studies and work hours precluded the usual ten-hour sleep cycle I maintained, even in college. It appeared that more judgments were made with limited information, and so I adjusted. I noted learning styles and interactions different from my experience at college. I reminded myself of the slogan for weary medical students, "P = MD." A pass will ultimately achieve the same medical diploma. There were assurances that every classmate would be supported and graduate with a medical degree. But I saw my first year roommate struggle. She decided not to continue the gauntlet run of medical school and chose to be a writer.

I experienced more diversity in our classes and clinical clerkships. I had been raised with the sameness of a Caucasian, Christian community. Only a sliver of David Thomas's paradigm for managing diversity existed in my childhood world. At age twelve, I had my first bagel with cream cheese and lox at the prompting of my friend's father. I also experienced a family member conspicuously avoiding interaction with a Muslim boyfriend of mine. Generational cultural shifts leading to inclusion slowly expanded in many realms. I continued to lead my life and maintained a relationship on the weekends. I married between my first and second year of medical school. Some classmates were unaware I had a boyfriend. University housing, which my father arranged as a wedding present, became home. These were the same university apartments in which I had first resided as a newborn.

During a pathology lab, a professor was pointedly quizzing students about the structures in the heart. As a person who had never responded well to this pimping or grilling style, I was totally taken off guard when I had a question barked at me. "What is your name?" I got out my first name, but I couldn't come up with my new married name in front of several classmates. The tittering began. The professor lightened up. I blurted my name out for the first time. Later in my career, I would draw attention to a youthful hospitalist that he was inappropriately grilling me. He appeared to believe this was not an unusual interaction style toward a more senior female emergency physician. Upon returning home to visit with high school friends, one former classmate would exclaim, "You are married to 'God's son!'" He had taken classes with my father-in-law. I had only a limited understanding that he was an internationally renowned veterinary professor. A future colleague would inquire about this man and his publications, receiving one as a gift from me. The interconnectedness of my worlds (high school, college, and medicine) was apparent.

Upon completing my second year of medical school in 1984, I added George Orwell's novel *Nineteen Eighty-four* to my extensive reading list of medical texts. Another landmark event during my second year of medical school was the diagnosis of a family member with juvenile onset diabetes. It appeared the condition was caused by excessive sugar intake, including packages of cookies and boxes of donuts, and carbohydrate loading in general for triathlon training (Mei 2011) by this family member, who shunned alcohol due to a family history of alcoholism. My grandmother's voice was saying moderation again in my ear. Ironically, earlier in the pathology course, upon noting all the long-term complications that were associated with diabetes, I had counted my blessings that this illness did not run in my family. Our physician insinuated the cause of this individual's diabetes was probably a virus. Additional years of medical research and an American society with poor dietary habits added credence to my hypothesis and insight of excessive sugar intake contributing to the incidence of diabetes.

Additional hurdles for women in the workforce include not just high workloads and intellectual rigor but harassment as well. During one six-week clinical rotation in my third year of medical school, I worked at a community hospital with two … should I say infamous male residents. These two men had a reputation for womanizing and victimizing the nurses. I had no less than five women approach me in the first week to offer support and guidance in dealing with these two residents. I felt thankful to be married. These residents had only one dating exclusion: married women. They told me I had a very nice figure in certain clothes. Profanity was intermixed with most daily rounds. Remember, these superiors completed my evaluation. They had my destiny in their hands. At the end of this rotation, one of the residents was particularly crude. I was done with this behavior and stated, "Fuck off, ____." Let me tell you, profanity is much more effective if you use it selectively. The rotation ended. I had performed well above expectations with early shift arrivals, task completion including orders and notes without prompting, and excellent judgment. Apparently, my evaluation included a statement to the effect that if I could survive a rotation with these two residents, I could survive anything. The future would tell.

When I interviewed for residency positions in internal medicine, I looked geographically in the region where family lived. I selected several highly competitive programs but also a smaller program due to the proximity of family and our love for the outdoors. When presenting for this interview at clearly the weakest program on my list, the male chair of the department of internal medicine inquired early in our interaction, "How do you believe as a female physician, you will be able to complete an internal medicine residency program?" This comment seemed incongruent with the rising number of women in medical school gradually increasing from 1970 to reach parity (Feeney 2015). Women also make up almost half of all employees in the American workforce (DeWolf 2017), with organizations led by women outperforming their peers (Lang 2004). I felt stunned and dumbfounded by this blatantly discriminatory question. I made curt responses to all additional questions, grabbed a quick free lunch, and proceeded out of the community. In retrospect, I believe this chair may not have wanted me to rank this program as a married applicant because I might disrupt the scheduling process with a potential pregnancy.

"A calm and modest life brings more happiness than the pursuit of success combined with constant

restlessness. ... Where there's a will, there's a way."
(Albert Einstein, two short notes to a hotel messenger
in Tokyo for a tip, upon receiving news that he was to
receive the Nobel Prize in physics)

I felt relieved that the residency director at my eventual university
was holistic. He also had empathy for resident spouses and understood
the need for work-life balance. Ah, moderation. This acceptance of
personal lives with work lives was important to me. A high school
schoolmate was sexually assaulted during my residency years. At her
request, I joined and supported her in the emergency department. The
preceptor of teaching rounds was thoughtful and released me from
our session. This act of empathy was significant for both my friend and
me. Additional shared grief would ensue when the perpetrator, known
to a group of friends, subsequently committed suicide. This growing
epidemic touched me personally.

As a resident, staff recognized my efficient and decisive style. I was
informed through the grapevine by a friend of my father's, who was on
a community attending physician review committee, that I was one of
the most appreciated interns during my first year of residency for my
work ethic and completeness. I thoroughly enjoyed the emergency rotations that required more problem solving and offered a diverse patient
population. One emergency nurse exclaimed when I arrived for a shift,
"Thank God you are here. You know what you are doing." Many of my
colleagues dreaded this rotation.

An early event in my residency, when I identified a surgical emergency, was impressionable. Only after contacting two unavailable surgical interns, a disbelieving second year surgical resident, and a chief
surgical resident did the patient proceed to the operating room. The
surgical attending, fearing possible repercussions for a delay in care and
protecting the reputations of his four male residents, filed an incident
report suggesting that I held responsibility for the delay in care and
placed me under the scrutiny of the legal department. This became
an early sign of the boys' club and interdepartmental scapegoating. I

spoke to the chief of the emergency department as he completed the incident-related quality review. The first surgical intern was doing his banking. The second surgical intern knew the first intern would be back in an hour and believed the delay was minimal. The surgical resident was uncertain of the severity of the patient's condition. The chief surgical resident was experienced enough to have the conviction to proceed immediately to definitive care in the operating room.

The administrator smiled at me and encouraged me to keep up the good work. He taught me to always do what was right for the patient. Miscommunications could be reviewed at another time. I would discover later in my career that doing the right thing did not always lead to non-judgmental discussions subsequently. I felt aghast that my judgment and career could be impugned by another service's attending surgeon without even hearing my perspective. This would not be the only time in my career that my character and reputation would be impugned during interdepartmental disputes while circling the wagons around the boys' club. Integrity was not a universal value. Poor patient outcomes did happen. Reviews to find root causes and improve processes are essential.

Most of my rotations as a resident were enjoyable, but my favorites were in the emergency department. I felt I had the largest impact on patient care. I problem solved for a probable diagnosis and initial treatment plan. The Dalai Lama and Pope Francis have also lauded the need for good problem solving. Another fellow resident found his eventual path to a career in intensive care. As we coincidentally ended up on the same plane traveling to different work-related events, he told me that he pursued a career in critical care because I made his internship rotation enjoyable as his supervising second-year resident.

> "Complaining not allowed. Whiners may lose their sense of humor and ability to solve problems. So, stop complaining and act to make your life better." (Pope Francis's sign at his Vatican residence)

Another memorable experience occurred on an elective rotation in the dermatology clinic. The rotation included working with a fine senior attending physician seeing several patients with acne who received Accutane prescriptions. With my biopsychosocial bent, I wondered whether maybe pregnancy tests should be checked out of the utmost precaution with a relatively new medication that may have adverse effects on fetuses. These teenage girls were clearly interested in improving their acne for social appeal and dating relationships. Later that same year, this testing became standard practice for the specialty. Fresh eyes on common conditions and management often see new concerns and possibilities. This proved true when I changed positions between hospitals. However, not all administrators saw this opportunity for new insights by fresh eyes.

There were opportunities to demonstrate my problem solving in a primary care physician's office. I saw a patient with new abdominal pain and proceeded to write a transfer note to the hospital emergency department, including my diagnosis and plan. The supervising attending was impressed with what proved to be an accurate diagnosis after only a short encounter with no data and no prior history. Similarly, I demonstrated empathy for a depressed patient who was experiencing derogatory comments from her counselor regarding her religious values, coping mechanisms, and support systems. This attending physician accepted my concern and the patient's perspective. This patient's care continued without any further interaction with the unhelpful counselor.

Throughout my training, there were opportunities to share empathy with patients experiencing physical and mental pain. Uncertainty and confusion abound for patients and providers alike. Each medical rotation highlighted a different patient population with the universal need to be heard and understood. Empathy and alleviation of suffering are the goals (Morse 2008). Staff members and colleagues also sought empathy for experiences of high workloads, emotionally draining encounters, and physical exhaustion. Humankind needs empathy and hope for resilience.

I also connected with my own physicians in a different fashion as I entered the profession. I had an amazingly kind ophthalmologist who would review eye charts with me. As I struggled, he would encourage me to "just try" to read any letters I could decipher. I paused and took the chance for a teachable moment. I explained to him that I possessed an extremely competitive personality with an impeccable work ethic. The mere insinuation that I might not be trying was very painful for me. Might he believe me when I said I could not see any recognizable letters and proceed to a larger screen? He was soft-spoken and kind. Our visit completed. I was immensely impressed when a year later, this same ophthalmologist scrolled through the screens of letters, saying, "Stop me when you can recognize any letters." I would appreciate this man for this simple gesture. I would also later be part of his care at the end of his life, and I wished to provide every ounce of kindness to him.

During my last year of residency, I hoped to become pregnant and have a child between residency and my first position as an attending physician. I spoke to the residency director to make sure my require-ments would be met and I would miss no critical rotations. He was very supportive. He requested notification if and when I became pregnant. I felt fortunate and ecstatic to expect my first child in April. I beamed while showing my first ultrasound to an oncologist in the cafeteria. He politely showed joy for me. I rearranged all my night calls, which was arduous as a senior resident, to ensure I would not miss any during maternity leave. Much to my surprise, several male residents were an-noyed at this front-loading of my night shifts early in the year, because this implied they would have a few extra night shifts back-loaded in their schedules. Of note, the most vocal male residents had children at home already.

My internal medicine residency was completed in 1989. Moving out of a lifetime of training for a career in medicine was a dream come true. I enjoyed the intellectual rigor and the interpersonal interactions with a diversity of people.

"Emotion, attention, empathy, mindful meditation, compassion, not judgement, understanding, problem solving." (Dalai Lama)

The key lessons about empathy give me hope for the future.

Empathy—Caring

- There is no shame for finding yourself in a bad situation that you had no part in creating.
- Listen to feedback from those who sincerely care about your best interests.
- Choose mentors. Avoid detractors and opportunists.

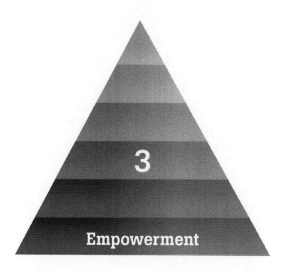

3

Empowerment

My adult life included medicine with clinical, research, and teaching responsibilities; my growing family; and a passion for changing the world. My faith and my desire to advocate for others became personalized with my own survivorship. At the completion of my residency in internal medicine, I decided to pursue a career in emergency medicine. I researched the opportunity and grandfather clause requirements for this relatively new specialty. I continued a university appointment when I worked at a community hospital for five years. I enjoyed teaching a course in which basic history and physical skills were taught in the clinical setting of community hospitals. I always enjoyed this opportunity to interact with students and refresh my skill set. I hoped to participate years into the future and teach the biopsychosocial model, a model of the connectedness of an individual's body, mind, and social health (Engel 1981).

Upon completing four of the five years of clinical practice required at an affiliated hospital, I approached an administrator of the university hospital to assist me with the board certification process. He stated he had no idea about the request to which I referred. Even as he told me this, I was aware he was assisting a male medical school classmate through this exact process. A letter was required in the application process. This administrator was known for making gender-biased statements that women should not be in medicine. He also had less knowledge of my work due to my affiliated hospital position. However, all my training was at this institution, and plenty of administrators could attest to my abilities. He was essentially refusing to write a recommendation letter to complete my board application. I immediately went to an administrator in the department of internal medicine, my specialty of training, but no action was taken on my behalf. I was unable to sit for the emergency medicine boards. My inability to demonstrate "appropriate" credentialing moving forward greatly impacted my career mobility to other institutions or communities, credibility for my chosen clinical practice setting, and future potential in my career of choice. I would be unable to retain or perceivably maintain leadership positions in emergency medicine.

The administrator blocking my career path was no longer in his position the following year, possibly in part to my personal story compiled with other stories unknown to me. This is not dissimilar to the collection of sexual assault claims that result in consequences for perpetrators when large numbers of events with similar stories become credible. I pursued no legal action at this juncture. I was a young attending physician, a mother of three preschool children, a primary breadwinner with a soul- and career-searching spouse. I had no time, resources, or interest for an extended legal interaction with the only academic medical institution in my community with whom I hoped to retain employment for decades to come. My father had completed his entire career in this community, and I hoped to do the same. The university had difficulty recruiting and retaining faculty without local connections. I falsely perceived that my personal ties to the community and talents would be welcomed and lauded for my career's duration.

A new female chairperson recruited me back to the university hospital in 1994 to assist as faculty for a new emergency department residency program. In retrospect, this gesture may have been a partial compensation for the university abandoning me with the board certification process. I was well aware through years of feedback that I had excellent clinical judgment. I appeared more efficient and thorough than my peers. Everyone has strengths and deficits. The disparity, which was easy to decipher, was between the staff who filled in your deficits to improve processes and those who collected your deficiencies to hold leverage, instill fear, and exert power over you (Inesi 2011; Lewis 2002).

I knew I would now need to entertain academic endeavors. Previously at the community hospital, I had learned about partner violence. I networked with the social workers to improve services provided to this patient population. I had offered to seek out a speaker for a community forum only to find I was the most knowledgeable physician in our vicinity at the time. I prepared a lecture and was met with questions and encouragement from medical students to bring this subject matter to the medical school. Now in my new position, I had the opportunity to teach and research interpersonal violence. This transition occurred in January 1994, months before the infamous car chase scene and murder trial of NFL icon O. J. Simpson.

There were some laughable moments when I returned to the university emergency department. The first week, I sat in my office setting up paper files and arranging text books. I was uncertain how to start with my computer. No computer science had been required when I'd completed my math major! I walked down a short hall to an open door and entreated a male colleague to assist me. He wandered back to my office, reviewed my set up, and realized I didn't know how to turn on my computer. College papers were written on a typewriter. He then turned on the power switch to the computer. He could have maligned me about my ignorance for years to come, but he did not. I published my first research article in JAMA two years later. Luck in timing played a part as the topic of partner violence peaked with the O. J. Simpson trial. Meta-analysis shows women (including me) acknowledge luck, whereas men are recognized for skill with successes (Swim 1999). I would interact with clients and staff at a local advocacy group to expand my knowledge of advocacy issues and my skill sets.

Once, when I gave a preliminary draft of a manuscript to the chair of the emergency department for comment, I felt dismayed. I discovered days later that I had misspelled a key word in the title and the entire manuscript. This was undeniable. With grace, the chair let it pass, knowing a future spell-check would remedy the situation. This manuscript made it to publication. One of my former community hospital colleagues was also launching into an academic career. He had joined the emergency medicine faculty within the year after my move to the university hospital. Although our research topics did not initially lend themselves toward collaboration, I attempted to launch an idea that led to a joint publication. He thanked me for this gesture of inclusion and support, which he noted had not been extended by any other faculty member to date.

As a young attending and director of the emergency medicine clerkship for fourth-year students, I participated on a clinical instruction committee. I lobbied strongly for a mandatory rotation in emergency medicine to foster better understanding of this young specialty with whom most physicians would interact in their careers. I watched the primarily senior male faculty members seem disinterested and unwilling to support my idea. Wonderfully, the medical school dean amplified my idea, chimed in that he thought this would benefit the student body, and pushed the motion over the finish line.

Emergency medicine publications acknowledge that amplification helps lessen bias against women. This mechanism attempts to buffer gender biases and struggles of women to make their voices heard in a male-dominated workplace with unconscious bias. When not embraced by men, amplification uses the collective voice of women when reiterating ideas or accomplishments of a single woman. Women colleagues, if available, work together and make each other's voices heard. This amplification starts the process to eliminate gender disparities that continue to persist by supporting diversity and inclusion of thought (Felton 2017).

One afternoon, I designed a restructuring of the emergency department charting document in about two hours. I then agonized for months to achieve acceptance by everyone who might conceivably have any input. The emergency department interacted with almost all other departments. The final result was a mostly unchanged document. I felt frustration for the protracted processes exacerbated by doubting individuals, partially based in unconscious gender bias. Future efforts often required a self-assured senior male faculty member to amplify my ideas for success (Lipman 2018).

On one medical school committee, members cast votes to elect students into the medical honor society. At one meeting, I felt publically ostracized. I was informed of my ineligibility to vote for new honor society members because I was not currently a member myself. This was despite my interaction with every single member of the student body as director of a mandatory rotation in the emergency department. Subsequently, a student body elected me into the medical honor society. The inconsistencies and lack of democratic values were apparent to me. All citizens could vote for president. Citizens from all backgrounds served on juries. This belief that only people "of quality" could recognize quality perpetuated old-school structures and memberships. The achievement of diversity is delayed and more protracted. Diversity fuels innovation, and yet people want to hire and recognize people like themselves (Comstock 2016). Later in my career, an authoritarian administrator would inform me our unit and department were not a democracy, in order to silence my voice. I would reflect on the likelihood of improved outcomes if all voices were heard.

On top of patient encounters, workplace interactions were noteworthy of human character. Most staff were kind and professional. On occasion, disrespectful remarks were made regarding tasks that appeared customer service oriented and unnecessary to these individuals. Ridiculing statements about ideals showed some individuals didn't value basic university tenants. Some staff clearly had difficulty with a female superior. On one occasion, when I attempted to amplify my own willingness to follow a consultant's guidelines and reach out to improve patient satisfaction, an administrator actually laughed at me. He described me as the only physician who complied with the guidelines; by deduction, I was the aberrant physician.

Social innuendos were part of the work environment. One male colleague referred to me as the Vanna White of the department early in my career because I almost always wore heels and a dress or skirt for my clinical shifts, as well as for my teaching and research activities. Similar to the famous dancer Ginger Rogers paired with Fred Astaire, I performed the same clinical tasks as my male colleagues—in heels. A female colleague once mentioned that she routinely attended an administrative meeting without the title or position of all the male attendees. Her confusion was cleared by a male attendee who actually admitted she was invited as a pleasant visual distraction for the men when the meeting became tedious and boring. Objectification of women for men's pleasure persisted.

Office space, or the lack thereof, would be a perpetual issue my entire career with at least four office location changes. I always requested one feature: a window. I shared an office with a doctor of pharmacy in our department for a few years. He was known to be gay and made some male physicians uncomfortable, at least when it came to sharing an office. The chair knew my tolerance for diversity and informed me the two of us would share an office. The space was unreasonably small because emergency departments were initially divisions of the department of internal medicine; no office space previously existed in the emergency area. I could not get from my desk to the door without my colleague standing up. He could not get from his desk to the filing cabinet without me standing up. This became reminiscent of my freshman college dormitory, with senior single rooms converted into freshman double rooms, but smaller. Fortunately for my office mate, I usually occupied the office after night shifts and stood to read my mail and complete work so I would not fall asleep.

At another point in my career, efforts to oust me from the department and make me miserable included providing an office space worthy of a corner closet. The space even included the department vacuum and extra telephone books. The administration appeared to track my work by following my use of this office space, to no avail. With no window, work proceeded elsewhere. Elements of manipulation and coercion became apparent with this institutional carrot and stick approach. The primary bargaining chips included salary, scheduling preferences, office space, and parking arrangements.

Throughout my career, some professionals would appear to throw me under the bus, broadcast humorous oversights, and maintain an antagonistic power and control structure. The academic community is no different than the community at large. Some individuals exhibit controlling behaviors to improve their sense of self. One male physician alluded to the perks of a career in medicine, including money, sex, and power. Money is tighter with healthcare reform efforts. In June 2018, the *Emergency Medicine News* listed persistent salary variabilities by gender, title, and practice locations. Sex at the workplace is no longer tolerated, as exemplified by the Me Too movement. Power and control are the bargaining chips for an already hierarchical work environment. The power and control dynamics of the community and households bleeds into even the hospitals. Some men treat women in this fashion because they can; there is little accountability.

I once was asked to give a lecture on short notice, in another city for a pediatric conference on violence. I had numerous prepared lectures on my research and teaching area of expertise, partner violence. I included general examples of presentations of patients I had cared for in my clinical practice. These lectures focused on various specialties, including primary care specialties, obstetrics, psychiatry, and emergency medicine. I directed a session on partner violence for the ambulatory care clerkship, my initial joy in teaching. I had also taught a humanities elective for years with readings on various forms of violence, including suicide, homicide, gun violence, partner violence, and child abuse. I assured the director of this conference that I would be glad to assist him on short notice. In fact, I coincidentally had a wedding in the same city that weekend, which would make travel less of a burden.

On Friday evening, I attended the wedding, reviewed my presentation, and turned in to bed early. I arrived at the conference at a reasonable time before my lecture, slated as the last lecture before lunch. My introduction by the course director went as follows. "I am sorry our previous presenter, a former patient of mine, could not be here today. Her personal experiences were always very insightful. She died last month. Here is Dr. …"

How had this information not been shared with me ahead of time? I was floored. Clearly the director felt my youthful appearance and social engagement the night before might limit my presentation. He was hedging to cover a potential disappointing last lecture of the morning session. Nonetheless, I approached the podium and transitioned, stating I shared the sadness that this patient could no longer share her health issues and personal insights. I acknowledged, as a physician, that our greatest lessons come from our patients. Then I proceeded with my lecture. I noted my surprise that a pediatric conference on violence had not already included the significant impact partner violence has on children in the home, my topic. Abusive behaviors are witnessed and learned by children in the home. I would suggest abusive behaviors are also witnessed and learned by staff and students in the workplace. The primary reason women stay in abusive relationships is to maintain a family and lifestyle for her children. Paradoxically, the primary reason women leave abusive relationships is to protect their children from the abuse learned (as both victim and perpetrator) or received by her children. This advocacy of mothers for their children is not dissimilar to immigrant mothers seeking asylum for themselves and their children. My lecture received a standing ovation and the subsequent attempt by the director to repair his insulting introduction as I received my speaker's fee and left the premises. This episode highlights the additional hurdles many women confront in their careers. Not only are women not amplified and lauded when speaking—in this instance as an expert on short notice—but they may be placed in a hole to dig out of before even uttering a word.

Another senior male faculty member sought to capitalize on my growing reputation and high energy level. He offered me a department title and his own research idea to assess the pathology of women who stay in abusive relationships. My head was screaming, "Run away!" Women stay in abusive relationships because of the perceived benefit for their children or because they lack the job, money, resources, and support to live independently. Mansplaining appeared to be in full view (Tobar 2014). I felt uninterested in the position with a predetermined agenda, and the offer was not revisited. A predominantly male research forum was eager to provide lots of research ideas, never acknowledging that I had plenty of my own ideas at that juncture. This cloning effect in mentoring, where promising students and junior faculty are brought up in the image of senior faculty, is "narrow sighted, personally motivated and not sensitive enough to the unique interests and vocational dreams" of the mentees (Johnson 2015).

Later in my career, efforts to improve initial assessments upon arrival to the hospital were entertained. I led the triage effort and came up with the idea of prompt assessment for quality; I liked the idea of minding your Ps and Qs. Alterations of this descriptor occurred at subsequent meetings with input from the chairwoman and nurse manger. These changes included shortening until presentation with the new e-record became PA. I felt mercilessly chided, and negative gossip went rampant about my vanity for naming a new operation process after myself by using my initials. This was not without some precedence with a prior medical director, but he had no audible backlash. This may seem trite, but the recurrent double standard for genders in the workforce was emphasized to me. As a woman, I felt vilified for the mere appearance of something self-aggrandizing that I did not do, whereas a man received a pass and recognition for actual self-promotion. Of note, men have named buildings and institutions after themselves for eternity. Consider the current example of Trump Towers.

Transfers to the floor from the emergency department were often fraught with tedious discussions. Upon recognizing this as a major talking point at a faculty meeting, I sought an improvement with the chief medical officer. He amplified my effort, and a new policy was created and distributed within the week. It was so nice to speak with a powerful individual who recognized an opportunity to improve processes and made it happen. Unfortunately, some individuals sought greater recognition. I simply wanted to further progress toward equality, quality, and efficiency. More episodes of pointing out flaws and tearing down occurred, rather than team building. There were several misrepresented encounters. I felt fortunate to have administrators who had known me for years as a student and resident; they trusted my penchant for the truth and my integrity.

> *"Courage—judgment—integrity—dedication—*these are the historic qualities ... which, with God's help ... will characterize our Government's conduct in the 4 stormy years that lie ahead."* (President-elect *John F. Kennedy*, address to the Massachusetts legislature, January 9, 1961)

In general, I was well received and promoted to assistant and associate professor over the next decade. Men and women of quality did not fear equality in the workforce. The unit staff approached me with gratitude and relief almost every shift. They frequently shared stories of suboptimal management from the prior day when staffed by another. Studies have found women are better at multitasking than men (Morgan 2013). Staff implored me to advocate for them to improve unit processes and interactions, which I did. I patterned my day to fit the desired metrics as a professional, not the minimalist shift worker. I rose at 4:00 a.m. to read all charts before arriving at work around 6:30. I transferred any unstable or inappropriate patients before the day shift arrived at 8:00. The team soon learned my rounding, orders, and notes would follow. Patients would be discharged mostly by noon to allow staff lunch and time to rev up for a new group of patients in the afternoon. On days staffed by others, patients might wait until the afternoon before being seen by a provider. The administrator even acknowledged once when we arrived by mistake on the same day, "The nurses were right: you have rounded before I even arrive." If a lull arose, there was teatime at 2:00 p.m. on Thursdays.

Happiness at work doesn't mean you are not working hard enough. It means you are effective. "The Happiness Advantage- Because positive brains have a biological advantage over brains that are neutral or negative, this principle teaches us how to retrain our brains to capitalize on positivity and improve our productivity and performance" (Achor 2010).

"Your competition isn't beating you because they are working more hours than you, it's because they are working smarter." (Robbins 2017)

"Survivors take great joy from even their smallest successes." (Gonzales 2004)

The key lessons about empowerment will carry into my future ambitions.

Empowerment

- Diversity improves organizational outcomes (Choo 2017). This may take some leaders out of their comfort zone.
- Individuals must choose their own priorities and destiny. Consequences are real for those who choose to push for equality. Similar to partner violence, each competent individual should make decisions for herself.
- All team members have value.
- Create win-win choices.
- You can only control your own actions.

4

Life Balance

Family and career balance was a struggle. Work-family imbalance is a top reason for leaving some careers (Fouad 2017). "Work hard, play hard" was a mantra I repeated to myself and my children, reminding them the work came first. I created chores and errands before playtime to instill work ethic. I thrived on the simple beauty and joy of life at home. Fortunately, my children were healthy. The largest hurdle was childcare in the preschool years. Although I did not utilize the hospital childcare facility, I saw this investment as a true asset.

I was pleased when an elementary school teacher was able to see the polarity of the temperaments of my children, rather than lumping them together as one household. My son preferred a place in the corner with a good book. My daughter preferred to interact and orchestrate. Many human resource personnel, similar to teachers, understand the need to treat employees as unique individuals. I cringed when the combined kindergarten and first grade class, in which I had a son and daughter, was called K-1. Coincidentally, this was the designation of the morgue at the university hospital.

My department chairperson had offered me a position unaware I had three preschool children. Women in all career paths encounter the "motherhood penalty" (Miller 2014). This is a term coined by sociologists who explain working mothers experience systemic disadvantages in wages, perceived competence, and benefits relative to childless women. This pay gap may even exceed the gap between men and women. Evaluations include statements of less commitment, less dependability, and less authoritarian attributes. One common theory is the work-effort theory. This penalty effects hiring, pay, promotion, and work experience. Shelley J. Correll notes, "Mothers were consistently ranked as less competent and less committed than non-moms."

This chairperson showed momentary regret, but that regret soon subsided. I had always been the busy person who got things done. In fact, my administrative assistant was snatched by this chairwoman after my exuberant praise. These individuals both were aware that a task not completed by me within forty-eight hours would surely need further clarification. I was often the trial case and one of the pacesetters for many department actions. Being the ideal worker was mythical (Carter 2011). I had a couch in my office for the occasional nap during an overextended day, a sick child, or an exhausted colleague.

When my children exuded empathy for their classmates and teachers, this pleased me. One day in elementary school, my daughter retold witnessing unidentified distress of her teacher. She told the teacher, "It will be okay." She also retold a disturbing event of one classmate mistreating another, representative of the bullying phenomena. I explained that lessons appear from all events in our lives. We would resolve to never inflict such pain on another person in this fashion ourselves. I would retell this story to a female chair after she sent a scathing e-mail, the contents of which were still unclear to me, bringing another colleague to tears.

> "Parents teach empathy the same way they help their children learn to talk." —Mary Gordon, founder of Roots of Empathy (Huffington, *Thrive*)

My youngest daughter sprang the mother surprise of my parenting years as her birthday approached. Our family celebrated birthday week because it was never clear if I would be working clinically on a given birthday. I tried to work the day shift, if feasible, in order to be home for dinner. One year my daughter was all excited for her birthday the next day. While being tucked in for bed, she announced the best part of a birthday at school was the mother came in to read a book of the child's choice. I was caught by surprise. I kissed her, left the room, and went into emergency mode. I called my mother and begged her to read a story to my daughter's class on my behalf. She agreed and dutifully read the selection of my daughter, *Are You My Mother?* (P. D.Eastman 1960). Psychotherapists, enjoy!

The joy of child rearing buoyed me to ignore much of the misbehavior in a tumultuous emergency department. I took the best of whichever world was moving more smoothly at any given time frame. Each environment was a reprise from the other. Some years the emergency department was a controlled environment compared to my household. Exercise broached fanatic with my spouse. Encouraging children beyond their athletic limits actually broke many children's bones. Injurious activities included rollerblading with the dog, scooters, rock climbing, thousands of round-offs in one day, tripping over the babysitter, striking the board while diving into a pool, and tumbling over a hurdle in a track and field event. I feared child protection might appear on my doorstep, except I was always at work during injurious episodes. As I pleaded to our pediatrician for my grandmother's tried and true moderation, I came to realize he also enthusiastically encouraged his children to excel in athletics.

One Christmas, a family member decided to broaden the toy selection at our home and gifted my son a Power Ranger. My son unwrapped the toy, noted the weapons, rose, crossed the room, and placed the gift in my hands. He did not cry or show anger. He simply knew I preferred no guns or violent toys in our home. He played with these toys at his friends' houses.

While arranging carousel slides for a lecture on partner violence, I would learn that my children's nanny was herself a survivor of partner abuse. Her stories were disturbing. I realized the close proximity of many individuals, unaware of significant details of each other's lives unless asked empathically with a direct question. Career paths crossed with a fellow childhood school bus rider in my neighborhood. We discovered we had a mutual teaching and research interest.

One daughter preferred to interact with her environment. If she was not in my presence, she was running water and flooding a room somewhere in the house. She joined the swimming and diving team at the university and was recognized as one of ten athlete scholars in 2012. I wrote an embarrassing brick on campus for her graduation: "Happy in water." Her brother had an equally sentimental brick: "Fun Competitor." Earlier in my daughter's childhood, while suffering from a broken arm, she received ketamine for the fracture reduction. She exclaimed that my colleague performing the sedation had four eyebrows; it was a prominent feature with just two. She also remarked, "I like this feeling," striking fear of future substance abuse in a physician mom's heart.

Gender issues were not absent in this time period. When my husband and I bought a house, I requested to be listed first on the mortgage as the primary wage earner. The banker assured me more than once that the order of names on this document was inconsequential. I persisted and stated that if that in fact were the case, the banker could provide me the courtesy, which would make me immensely happy. This later became a huge benefit to me during the stress of a divorce a several years later; there was no need to reapply for a mortgage.

> "Nevertheless, she persisted." (Senate Majority Leader Mitch McConnell admonishing a lengthy speech by Senator Elizabeth Warren, February 2, 2017)

> "If money is the difference between a future of security and comfort and a future of doubt and fear; if money is a major factor in your personal happiness; if money is a reflection of how you value and perceive yourself … Why don't you take better care of your money?" (Suze Orman, *Women & Money: Owning the Power to Control Your Destiny*)

There was also a credit card incident. While attending a work-related conference in December, hotel registration staff informed me my hotel bill would exceed my card credit limit. I had done my holiday shopping on this same card before traveling to the conference. I requested my credit limit be raised but was instructed I would need my spouse to make this request because he was the primary card holder. This blew a gasket for me. I had applied for all our credit cards, but the company had listed my spouse's name first. Needless to say, I chose a different credit card for this transaction, canceled the incident card, and moved on as a wiser woman.

Seemingly uncommon and unlikely events would come to pass in my adult years. I would tell myself, *Someday I must write a book.* This eventuality occurred sooner than I anticipated. I felt surprised on more than one occasion at the lack of compassion and empathy for colleagues if any event impacted the schedule and clinical load of other staff. As noted, I intended to work to support my household, and I did need diversion from personal tragedies at times. The implication that everyone would respect the schedule regardless of any ensuing events was often painful. Many events in my life also highlight the true benefit of a family leave policy to assist employees and families in times of need. Resources for employers to meet the needs of female employees exist (Zarya 2016).

After President Clinton took office in January 1993, the Family and Medical Leave Act (FMLA) of 1993 was the first major piece of legislation that he signed into law. The FMLA is a national labor law requiring covered employers to provide employees with job-protected and unpaid leave for qualified medical and family reasons. Qualified medical and family reasons include pregnancy, adoption, foster-care placement of a child, personal or family illness, or family military leave. Many citizens hoped that FMLA coverage would steadily expand to protect a greater number of workers and ultimately include wage replacement. There has been significant progress at the state level, and most family leave advocates continue to work toward the ultimate goal of a national policy. Family leave policies are gaining traction as prominent CEOs including Mark Zuckerberg avail themselves of these policies. The concept of life balance and family happiness impact work productivity and customer satisfaction in a positive fashion. Many international work environments have embraced family leave policies, but American culture continues to resist in many professions.

For a couple years, I endured a divorce and single parenting. This is difficult for anyone. As I contemplated the divorce, I spoke with a counselor about the loss of hopes and dreams. One of the biggest events in my childhood was my grandparents' fiftieth wedding anniversary. I adored both of them and cherished the happiness of their big day. I acknowledged, "I will never have a fiftieth wedding anniversary."

The counselor's helpful response, "You don't want to," was on target. Enough issues including anger, religion, money, interaction styles, coping mechanisms, time priorities, and the threat of infidelity made my marriage unsustainable. Life balance was two different concepts for my spouse and me. Happiness was two different goals.

Despite these real-life circumstances, patient care was paramount and quality was maintained. The ability to compartmentalize situations, handle emergencies, and move forward was innate to me. Unfortunately, I no longer possessed the protection of my married status, as I had enjoyed as a student and resident. Some unwanted male resident interactions occurred. One resident told me he loved me in a foreign language during a clinical shift. Another resident invited me to join a group at a strip club after a clinical shift.

Life can't throw just one hurdle at you at a time. While suffering a painful divorce, I needed to pass an alternate emergency medicine board exam to have some credibility in the field I wished to practice for my career. Although not recognized in all states, this credentialing would show I had attained some level of expertise to the disbelievers. I often studied at night after the children were in bed. As time pressures became more imminent, I encouraged each child to read his or her own book, while I read mine. I reviewed a series of case studies when my daughter pointed to the picture of an abdomen impaled with a knife. I was taken aback that my daughter was reading my book and not hers. I explained that bad things could happen to people, and I needed to know how to help these individuals.

The credentialing exam was offered out of my state. Rather than proceeding to the second portion of the exam, which seemed more emotionally taxing for me, two days after the written portion, I traveled to see a family friend who lived in the area and could console me over my pending divorce. Nonetheless, I assisted my two male colleagues for a bit. I had done much more outlining of the process in preparation with key actions required to pass. I rescheduled my own exam a couple months later. I passed but not without some intrigue. I was unaware that the presumption for testing administrators in this session was that attendees had failed the exam during the prior date aligned with the written exam. I crossed paths with a female colleague who had transferred to another institution. She smiled at me with a sorrowful but supportive expression. I felt no need to explain. Life happens, and it's complicated. Never complain. Never explain. My career would also be intertwined with the two male colleagues who were seeking emergency medicine credentialing. We shared future research and clinical duties.

Health issues happen to health professionals and their family members. My current spouse had rarely accessed primacy care and preventative care prior to our marriage. He is independently employed, and the cost was exorbitant. He had blood in his stool. I encouraged him to see his primary care physician and ultimately have a colonoscopy. He was diagnosed with colon cancer, which was completely resected with curative surgery. On the day after his surgery, while working in the emergency department, my spouse's primary care physician called to discuss the care of a mutual patient. He was surprised that I was at work. Changing the clinical schedule or missing a clinical shift work was severely frowned upon. In emergency medicine, the expectation was that a physician would only miss work on short notice if one was on one's death bed.

My infrequent personal episodes of health lapses were met with significant disbelief and a need to justify my dire condition beyond a doubt. There was always a solicitation for more personal information that seemed inappropriate. On one rare episode, I felt so weak that I could not get out of bed to take a shower. I had juice and water at the bedside. I had drenching sweats. I made an appointment with my physician and implored her to call in sick for me, which she did. I felt more connected to my physician when she revealed her similar desire to advance the position of women in society. She was the first female member of an established local golf club in the community. The club had wanted to maintain their tradition of only male members, but she explained her husband was not even a golfer. Unfortunately, this fine physician felt undervalued and moved her practice out of state.

On another occasion, while working a night shift, I felt nauseated but functioning. In the wee hours of the night, my symptoms worsened. I was almost through the night. In no way would I have any relief staff until shift change at seven. I had a nurse provide a dose of a nausea medicine and a bag of fluids. I completed the shift. Not unlike the entertainment world, the show must go on.

During all these exhausting years, I always admired a male physician who had completed a career in surgery. He dedicated himself to a second career in emergency medicine and teaching. He had an impeccable work ethic and spent time with students and residents, providing surgical pearls and history lessons. He always inquired about each individual's interests. I would remind myself that if this man, who'd educated my father and me, could present to work every day as he did, then so could I. I hoped to spend my latter years following this man's lead and sharing clinical pearls and encouragement with future students and residents. He celebrated his ninety-ninth birthday with many appreciative colleagues and students. He lived until 103 years of age, mentally intact.

> "For many men, work defines who they are, and they still need to benefit from something meaningful and productive as they age, whether it's in their current job or field or something new," says Dr. William S.

Pollack, assistant clinical professor in the Department of Psychiatry at Harvard Medical School. "Work can boost confidence, self-esteem, and happiness, all of which can help men stay active and live longer." (Pollack 2016)

I wonder, what about women?

Years later, I was struck by a car while seated in a salon by the storefront window. The driver was an elderly man who'd accidentally hit the accelerator while parking. I catapulted out of my chair and into the reception desk. I suffered a facial laceration, broken cheekbone, and bodily aches and pains. I missed one week of work and two clinical shifts, dubbed as vacation. Unscheduled time off is severely rebuked in shift work environments, including medicine. The departmental staffing structure appears to limit flexibility for unanticipated absence. Leadership initially portrayed me as a slacker who was letting down the team. Now granted, details of the episode were not fully known until the business owner offered the storefront video, which I shared with the female medical director, and the facial CT scan was completed a couple weeks later. But that made it feel worse for me. My integrity and work ethic were questioned due to my inability to work clinically, even after decades of service to the emergency department.

A similar sense of interrogation arose after an injury when I incorporated exercise into my household chores. I missed a stair rounding the basement door and tumbled to the cement floor. I failed to grab the side rail because I held a cup. Later, the resident orthopedist would try to sort out the potential for partner or family violence in my visit for a complicated upper arm fracture. He did not ask a direct question. I resolved to remain the patient rather than seize the teaching opportunity for partner violence, which would involve asking some of the following questions.

- Has anyone close to you made you feel unsafe? Do you feel safe at home?

- Has anyone close to you insulted you frequently, isolated you from friends or family, frequently embarrassed you, or withheld financial resources such as food, medication, shelter, or any other basic needs?
- Have you ever been pushed, grabbed, shoved, or slapped?
- Have you been kicked, bit, choked, or hit with a fist?
- Has anyone forced you to have sex that makes you feel uncomfortable?

The attending orthopedist remarked my injury was often life-changing at a follow-up visit. I showed her my nearly full range of motion, which was unusual six weeks after this injury. I swam daily, even doing a modified backstroke. This was not nearly as impressive as the 2018 lanterne rouge in the Tour de France, Lawson Craddock. At the time of the injury, a medical administrator questioned me about the severity of the injury with a tone insinuating I was capitalizing on the injury for time off. I missed one week of work and two clinical shifts—another week dubbed as vacation. The orthopedic physician assistant at my two-week follow-up was surprised I had already returned to work. The double standard for physician, now injured patient, was apparent.

I continued to place a positive spin on seemingly negative experiences. After this severely broken arm, I delighted in the opportunity to have lunch with my husband after an extended emergency visit. I also portrayed a joy of evening shifts to my children, especially in their high school and college years. We gathered at midnight for wings and a beverage of choice (Diet Coke for me). Little did they know, much later, that I was a morning and day person who required ten hours' sleep to be fully rested. I reframed my biorhythm for a career in an around-the-clock specialty plagued by sleep deprivation.

Social disaster beyond my divorce also tested my resilience. In an effort to ease me back into the dating world, my mother introduced me to a general contractor and handyman. He was portrayed as a single parent performing some household painting for my parents. The dating relationship was short but not without intrigue. This man was gracious and always bent to my preferences. He asked funny questions about my house and the household schedule. On occasional brief outings, he would touch base with work associates on the phone. I actually tried to create conflict once, but I could not provoke this man. He showed me pictures of his children but preferred to keep them at a distance due to the uncertainty of any long-term relationship.

My rational mind, with a sense of prevention and crisis management, was on high alert. Finally one night, my subconscious sorted out this relationship in my sleep. This man did not want a relationship. What did he want? I woke up from a dead sleep in a cold sweat. He was going to rob my house. How would he get in? Maybe the doors, but I had an alarm system. I proceeded around the house to find approximately ten previously locked windows were cracked open. He also intended to steal my car from the grocery store parking lot. The car keys were copied when I worked. Neighbors told me of a work truck in the driveway. I confronted this person and probably put my well-being at risk. I notified the police, locked the windows, changed the locks on my house, and bought the Club for the car.

Of note, I missed no clinical shifts or work time. My productivity still surpassed my colleagues. My usually appropriate female chairperson told me I could be manic but not depressed. She implied I might be bipolar, which I am not—and neither is my identical twin! I perceive myself as a highly effective type "A" personality with interval disappointments in life. One supportive male preceptor reassured me that this personality quality was an asset in a career in medicine. Psychiatric illness is often applied as a stigma to unaffected individuals who befall tragedy, or it's used to discredit them. This stigma is addressed in modern culture with Claire Danes's character Carrie Mathison, a single mother and CIA case officer, in the award-winning drama *Homeland*. Female politicians also experience this phenomenon.

> "As a prosecutor, Kamala Harris's doggedness was praised. As a senator, she's deemed 'hysterical.'"
> The Republican chairman of the Senate intelligence

committee admonished Senator Kamala Harris
(D-Calif.) during her questioning of Rod Rosenstein,
June 7, 2017. (Mettler, *Washington Post*, June 14, 2017)

Keeping the saga going after the initial disbelief of my parents, I informed them their house was probably the initial target; my house was merely a side job. When my grandmother died, my father took the precaution of having a neighborhood child stay at the home for the funeral service. This child's parents had raised concerns and came to our home themselves. Upon the hour of the funeral service, a knock came to the front door for a nondescript reason. The neighbors visualized a moving van parked slightly up the street, which moved on after they answered the door. Cassandra was on target one more time. Some circumstances were visible even without optical correction of glasses or contacts.

Upon remarrying, I took a personality test prior to marital counseling sessions. The senior priest informed the group of four couples that I was the only person he had ever seen with an equal distribution of responses across all four personality types. I responded that I interacted differently based upon my role in any given situation. I provided an example for the class of misinterpretations between couples. My husband has a beautiful voice. I would find myself listening to the tone but missing the words, frustrating him that I was not listening. In actuality, I listened to him lovingly. Similarly, an educational work video demonstrated this singular focus of many individuals. The video requested viewers count the passes or bounces of a basketball. During this engagement, a gorilla walked through the room and beat his chest. Those individuals intent on the math of counting, including me, totally missed the gorilla (Simons 1999). Teamwork and an understanding of diverse skill sets and predispositions are important.

Life was improving with a new spouse and partner in life, but I stumbled again. Financial issues of a blended household with six children and my spouse's bankruptcy due to poor investment decisions ensued. I had to seek a new mortgage in my name for our house. Upon remarrying, I moved into my spouse's residence because he taught piano lessons at home. He also had extensive piano technician equipment in the garage. This transaction occurred more rapidly when my mother-in-law retold the story of a distant relative burning down his house when confronting similar financial disaster. Every burner left on accidentally, and a preset oven setting, was unnerving. The fire department did arrive on more than one occasion. A pot left on the stove and an overcooked steak filled the first floor with smoke. Our next-door neighbor was a retired firefighter, and so help always arrived quickly.

I knew I had a passion for hard work, and I always planned on working, so I just carried on. At one point in my career, a male administrator unsuccessfully prodded me for my spouse's income. In hindsight, this administrator appeared to be assessing the financial condition I might be left in if I was precipitously unemployed to assuage any potential guilt he might be feeling. Many men still hang onto the role of men as the financial provider (Verel 2012).

Projecting happiness for my family was paramount. My license plate 'CFN' became the 'Certified Fun Network'. I enjoyed 'Words with Friends'. When driving I noted the great palindromes and number combinations on my odometer. Sometimes I took pictures to document the rare and exhilarating arrangements for anyone with whom I texted, not while driving.

The key lessons about life balance will carry into my future retirement.

Life Balance

- Keep a positive outlook.
- Be resilient. Failures are opportunities to learn. Success may be simply averting harm.
- Pick your struggles wisely.
- Issues that matter cannot be silent.

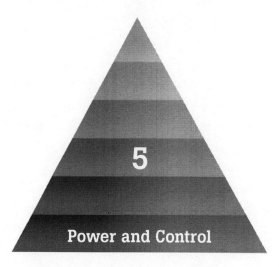

5

Power and Control

The overarching concepts that crush or empower individuals in society in general and the workforce in particular are presented in the next two chapters. Two pyramids, the action pyramid and the conflict pyramid, are visual representations of the complex nature of interpersonal relationships and group dynamics (see Graphics, page 94). Inclusive behaviors create a welcoming culture, whereas tribalism creates a hostile work environment. The action pyramid has a foundation of listening to all individuals, demonstrating respect, fostering inclusion and teamwork, amplifying all contributions, expressing tolerance and empathy, and seeking equity and empowerment through fairness and shared decision making. Differences of opinion are approached with education and a desire for common understanding. Mutual respect allows the ability to respectfully disagree. Contrary to the action pyramid, the conflict pyramid represents the negative behaviors that lead to conflict in the work setting and relationships in general. These pyramids provide a framework for reviewing the interactions I describe in the ensuing chapters.

There was a chaotic period of multiple chairperson turnovers in the emergency department. In 2009, the administration offered me an interim chairperson position. I declined. My spontaneous response was, "That's not going to work." I had been offered a couple of administrative positions but knew without my emergency board certification, blocked in 1993, I would be viewed by colleagues as unqualified. I lacked credibility for those who possessed this credentialing distinction. Also, research has shown men benefit substantially more than women by being the boss, in terms of autonomy as well as influence (Koenig 2011). I felt content with my various academic endeavors and sought to complete my career with the university. I offered the name of the subsequent chairperson whom I believed the faculty would follow.

Following my declination of the interim chairperson position and a contentious contract dispute, I appeared unwelcome. Typical operational issues and differences of opinion became my deficits and inadequacies. I documented this misrepresentation in real time with a professional e-mail to the appropriate administrator. Interactions were fewer. Sad, downcast eyes or averted eye contact revealed I was flagged as on my way out. Body language can be loud and clear. Jeff Thompson, a professor at Lipscomb University, describes the language beyond words for mediation, daily negotiations, and debates. My senior position and excellent service for years appeared disregarded.

I transitioned a portion of my clinical practice to an affiliated community hospital. I joined a new, two-physician unit consisting of a male administrator and me. The university emergency department administrator, in his position unknowingly due to my suggestion, apparently advised the observation administrator at the community hospital to not hire me. I had already secured a verbal agreement. I perceived this action as further retaliation after the contract dispute. With prior department restructuring, my medical director position disappeared. I had politely asked this newly minted chairman what role I might pursue. His response was an emphatic "Nothing." At the exact moment in time that the medical center valued my contributions and offered me the chairperson position, the subsequent chairman insinuated my total worthlessness. My emotional instincts were on target. Department efforts for me to repay clinical shift hours were not successful after contract renegotiations. Effective negotiating skills might be an asset for a team member in a work environment fraught with high-intensity interactions and perpetual staffing shortages. Apparently this skill may become a liability if you are a strong woman in a male-dominated work environment.

Upon transfer from the university hospital to an associated community hospital, my past and present contributions were seemingly regarded as irrelevant. I witnessed hospital leaders reach out to shake hands with new male physicians at quarterly staff meetings, beginning the inclusion and retention process. I did not experience this gesture or energy. How early in the process of new employment does the perception of fitting in, or not, become apparent? I had knowledge and skills to share in my new position. In a prior position, I triaged up to sixty patients in twelve hours. A chief resident with experience at another institution even commented to leadership that I was the only attending physician who ran the triage process as intended. Surely I could run a nine- to thirteen-bed unit in eight hours. Limited, occasional student teaching sessions or observations reminded me of my more connected and productive years. I attempted to include a colleague in these valuable teaching opportunities. He responded, "I am too cynical."

I was grossly underpaid for the first year of this new trial position despite staying in the university system. Only after one full year, transitioning all my clinical hours to this affiliated hospital and receiving positive feedback and a salary increase, did I provide feedback. I brought to the attention of the administrator of the emergency department that the emergency observation unit was perceived by unit staff to run more smoothly under my supervision. I offered to partner with the current administrator, who had no prior administrative experience. I had previously successfully administrated several medical school clerkships and clinical environments. This seemed like an easy fix with my problem-solving approach to improve unit processes and metrics. Any fair partnering of our skill sets and resources, including salaries, was subsequently portrayed as a power grab on my part. Most male leadership was unaware of positions I had declined due to an inability to effect change without the appropriate credentials denied due to prior gender discrimination. I had received the salary I required for parity with myself, working similar clinical shifts at two hospitals affiliated with the same institution and receiving two disparate hourly rates. This change did not even broach the idea of gender equality and "Equal Pay for Equal Work." I thought the salary discrepancy between me and the male administrator must be considerable for such a powerful slap-down.

> "Compensation has also lagged behind the progress women have made in participation in the workforce. In 2010 women were paid 77 cents for every dollar their male counterparts made." (Hegewisch 2012)

> "It is difficult to get a man to understand something when his salary depends upon his not understanding it." (Upton Sinclair, *The Jungle*)

The persistence of gender inequality is an issue addressed recently in emergency medicine publications. Authors acknowledge many inconvenient truths: women are still undervalued and underpaid; it is gender bias to not see women in leadership positions; "discoveries" are missed without women at the table; skilled professional women need to prove themselves to colleagues, superiors, and subordinates, unlike male counterparts; women tend to be better listening and communication skills; and implicit biases exist (Silverman 2017).

Gender issues have persisted throughout my career in the emergency department. An off-service male intern blatantly ignored me when I spoke with him about inappropriate military trench pictures (black humor for the job description in the emergency department) on an office doorway that was visible to all staff and patients in a clinical area I directed. This issue escalated to the residency director, who appeared to give some credence to this disruptive insubordination to a senior female physician. Later in my tenure in this position, I reallocated resources in my venue in a favorable fashion to this same service. The chairman of this service severely scolded me in a loud voice in front of two additional staff members. He arrogantly stood over me and accosted me for making any decision regarding his service, even if it was favorable and was an area I directed. He subsequently sent a polite apology. This is reminiscent of President Trump reprimanding his cabinet members in full display of others to exert his control. The negative effects of public criticism are difficult to repair. At the time of this incident, I laughed it off in the hallway and chalked it up to typical misogyny.

One medical administrator at the community hospital had difficulty interacting with senior female staff. Several nurses reported difficulties to a nurse manager but were dissuaded from filing a report with human resources. Subsequently, this manager who had attempted to address personnel issues sought alternate employment and departed from the community. Despite being a two-physician unit with a male administrator of similar age, training, and experience, he did not perceive me to be a peer, colleague, or team member. "You are not on the leadership team." He also aligned with the university male administrator, who discouraged my initial hiring at the community hospital, solidifying the boys' club and tribalism. This old-school mentality extended to previous generations and family members, some of whom made generous donations to secure potentially tenuous positions. Vestiges of pay to play in the university and medical system appear to remain.

The male administrator of the department generalized most conflict with alternate services when speaking solely with me. He recognized process issues and prior personal difficulties with some of the same individuals from which complaints arose and stated, "No big deal." The complaints were perceived as normal issues in a busy emergency department and a new unit routinely managed by leadership, after brief discussion with the employee and review of all pertinent perspectives. However, he switched horses and completely agreed with the male administrator, casting blame on me in any encounter with three or more people. Evolutionary psychology states you must act fast because there is a small window to act against abuse. Psychologically, dysfunction becomes the new normal. Narratives drift. Others go along

and adapt. Resistance becomes more difficult with time, even dangerous. The entire male leadership team had individual and collective
reasons—mostly power and control and distribution of work—for disregarding my perspective despite my superior clinical performance,
patient satisfaction, and unit staff satisfaction. I outperformed the male
administrator. He would not provide performance data. I adhered
to the university mantra of "ever better." There is always room for
improvement.

There was no woman or female administrator to amplify my message. I felt marginalized. There were rare observation unit meetings—
every four to six months, and none for two years prior to the consequential general discussion. After six years as the highest performer of
the two-physician unit to which I contributed since its inception, there
were hospital staff that moonlit in our unit and did not even recognize
my name. I would learn the unit administrator randomly changed
patient criteria on his shifts to be flexible, posted unit notices outside
the unit never provided to me, and provided summary documents for
moonlighters never reviewed with me.

I had no unit or hospital team despite university TEAMSTEPPS
educational programs. I explained that complaints and confusion were
a result of inadequate information sharing with all stakeholders of new
EOU policies, including patient criteria and standards of care. These
leaders were either woefully unprepared for administrative roles or
intentionally setting me up for more complaints to fuel a negative narrative. There appeared to be no interest or attempt to address issues in
a timely manner in order to improve processes and interdepartmental
relations. I explained to these two emergency physicians that they were
my team. My organizational structure was rejected. This dysfunctional
relationship parallels relationships at grander levels like the United
States being unable to recognize Canada as an ally in trade negotiations.

The lack of a voice for me was not subtle. There were no routine meetings for a newly formed unit. There were department meetings, but no unit issues of significance were appropriate in this venue.
Meetings with leadership were solely to provide negative feedback

without efforts to hear perspectives or solutions—no "sandwich technique" for these events (see Appendix: Effective Feedback, page 103). Complaint sessions were introduced with, "I do not want to hear your response. This is not a process issue."

Efforts at e-mail dialogue were perceived as inflammatory and annoying. I received direct statements of "I do not want to hear," like a husband to a demure wife, as well as orders to stop an e-mail chain and even "We will meet when I return," like a father coming home to admonish his children. These were staggering to me as a senior physician with extensive communication skills and awareness of power and control dynamics. I had spent decades on research and teaching about partner violence and sexual assault. I wrote down administrator comments in real time as a paper trail of inappropriate behavior toward me. Patterns of control may include emotional tactics, coercion, threats, intimidation, financial aspects, isolation and minimization, denial of events, casting blame, physical abuse, sexual abuse, and male privilege. The power and control wheel by the Domestic Violence Intervention Programs is an excellent illustration of elements of abusive relationships. I was denied a voice with repetitive discouragement over my input. Leadership reminded me I was not a part of the leadership team. My only defense was an occasional written document of my perspective when incidents were brought to my attention.

> "The most important thing for women … is to realize that any time they speak out they are going to have attacks leveled at them. Let's face it: our culture still isn't comfortable with outspoken women." (Ariana Huffington, journalist and *Huffington Post* cofounder)

I would seek out a female observation physician at another hospital. We would have networking lunches as an interval event to provide information, support, and potential career opportunities. The female department administrator and nurse manager would acknowledge my contributions with a gift coffee cup when the male leadership was notably on vacation. The male tribalism was in full force and led by the administrators in the emergency department. I do not believe all women experienced the same treatment. I did not experience this ostracizing myself until a male colleague felt threatened and I did not conform to the subservient style of some colleagues to one admitting hospital service. I wished to raise the bar for emergency physicians in general and female physicians in particular regarding respect and equity. I believe administrators unethically chose staffing goals, and staff fell in line. Administrative messaging about potential dismissal was clear to many employees.

I sought alternate positions in my prior university hospital and a new unit under construction at the affiliated, community hospital. Unfortunately, my options were limited in my current practice due to credentialing issues and perceived blacklisting by the university department leadership that controlled the smaller community venue. This included even the outlying hospitals that were affiliated with the university. Private practice for physicians is diminishing and much less common in emergency medicine. Human resources clearly manipulated information to the university's advantage, which did not adequately address the culture, actual behaviors, or individuals. I falsely perceived that my superior patient performance and deflection of tribal backstabbing would allow me to survive in this setting. I shared custody of my children and would be unable to leave the area.

I applied for the associate medical director position of the hospital, the highest physician position at the hospital. I was described as a strong candidate in a follow-up letter. Of note, during the initial group interview, I was addressed in an opening salvo as not credible. Maybe I would have been more credible if my academic title had not been removed from our unit brochure by a male physician with an inferior status, or if male colleagues acknowledged my contributions. Why did I need male leadership to deem me credible? To whom was I not credible? Surely not my patients, my unit staff, my students, or my co-authors. I had no poor patient outcomes due to my judgment and actions. I had teaching awards and numerous publications. I was involved in advocacy for others. I was a positive individual always striving to contribute and improve. Ah, "ever better." Even in defense of my credibility, listing my lifetime of accomplishments and laudable attributes was unseemly. My contributions were not assets to the organization, according to male leadership.

> "Women are sharing knowledgeable opinions and yet
> are not included or are straight up ignored." (Kass 2017)

There were so many episodes of failure to communicate. I do not believe this is a unique situation for me or the location in which I work. This is a power issue to silence feedback. Efforts to team build, provide all perspectives, and discuss process, instead of personalities with a diverse workforce, were rebuffed. I even gave a noon lecture on physicians criticizing other physicians to some of the most resistant individuals, including the administrator who was subsequently no longer in his leadership position. I raised my proclivity for nonviolence and my affinity for role models like Gandhi. Two men at this gathering actually made eye contact and volunteered while smirking that morning report comments about others were not true criticism. This venue clearly entertained routine, inappropriate, bashing comments. Those in power and control had no interest in entertaining a new perspective or sharing decision making. Everyone in leadership was comfortable with the status quo.

> "Every time we impose our will on another, it is an act
> of violence." (Gandhi)

> "What we have here is a failure to communicate." (*Cool
> Hand Luke* 1967)

> "While a national political system isn't quite the same
> as a marriage, it's built on the same foundation: a

commitment to shared values, a positive approach to conflict, strong communication." (Emba 2017)

"Behaviors such as poor coordination, conflicting information, blaming others, and disrespect are all signs of poor teamwork, which is associated with higher patient mortality and lower staff well-being." (McDaniel 2013)

Double Standard

"Do your part." (Admonishment by a medical administrator to resolve a work flow issue)

This phrase sounds insulting to someone who has excelled her entire career/life and silently goes the extra mile, above and beyond, every day to ensure quality care, efficiency, and staff satisfaction.

Dialogues are not challenges but attempts to find correct patient care plans and dispositions (discharge, observation, admission, consultation) for patients. This is the necessary process for appropriate patient care. Overworked and overwhelmed physicians may express frustration and hurt feelings when patient dispositions are changed. Individuals vent for stress relief. This may be allowed by leadership but is not often constructive or fact based. To alleviate time pressures for subsequent disposition efforts by these providers, brevity upon recognition of inappropriate dispositions to a given unit is desirable. Team building will alleviate individual emotions attached to these interactions that are not personal affronts. Education emphasizes team work for the proper care and disposition of each patient. There should be no animosity toward staff members.

Self-promotion or bragging appears unseemly for women. Self-promotion has been described as a risk factor for women (Rudman 1998).Unfortunately, this is a reality for women who have no female colleagues to amplify their message and laud their accomplishments.

Direct and efficient care provided in a high volume rapid turnover unit by a woman suddenly becomes noncollegial. Gender appropriateness is an unstated and unconscious bias.

Much of my life has been in a predominantly male environment, which is not an uncomfortable zone for me. As previously noted, I majored in math when girls were supposed to struggle with math. I attended a previously all-male university and celebrated ten years of women on campus. Female students spent much of our non-academic time equalizing the impact and voice of the female student body. I entered the career of medicine having spent my childhood being continually questioned about becoming a nurse. I practiced emergency medicine, which is predominantly a male field. I have been the primary wage earner for my children and household. I am the primary financial force for my family. Unlike prior generations, most women no longer work simply as a secondary or supplemental income, or as a hobby to keep their minds active. Why do women still have to struggle for recognition and advancement when it is apparent women excel in their professions?

> "Somehow it's unseemly for women to promote themselves. We think that there's a meritocracy that's hierarchical, and the people at the top make decisions about what promotions are based on." (Valerie Jarrett, Obama Administration senior advisor)

> "When there is unequal treatment, learn how to promote yourself in a way that is constructive … you can be factual about it." (Sheila Bair, FDIC chairperson)

> Self-promoting for a woman: "It's like having something deeply wrong about you. You sense this is a really bad thing." (Senator Elizabeth Warren)

My self-promotion was more disconcerting to male leadership than clear harassment and gender bias in the workplace brought to their attention in real time, both verbally and in writing. Ideas I suggested in my current clinical role were standard practices written in journals and discussed at national meetings. I expected no credit. These ideas were not my perspective but ideas presented at national conferences, such as the need for monthly (if not weekly) unit meetings. My goal was improved unit processes, team building, communication, and staff retention. Introductory management classes provide educational points: encourage ideas, input, dissent, and points of view; assist employees to feel a part of the organization; invest in process; and results require execution. Change at a large institution is like turning the *Titanic*. Active engagement continues (Pao 2017; Richards 2018). This smacks of the military attempting to confront gender discrimination.

> "To reach the upper levels of leadership, which create elite organizations, leaders must transition from producers to developers because people are any organization's most appreciable asset." (Maxwell, *How Successful People Lead*)

> When addressing sexual assault in the armed forces with sweeping reforms, Gillibrand, Senator from New York, stated "we have changed wholesale, the power the commanders have. We've turned the old system on its head." (Gillibrand 2014)

My expertise included advocacy, communication skills, shared decision making, and efficiency. I perceived myself as thorough and highly effective with an impeccable work ethic. Complaints are opportunities to improve and evolve. A direct, brief, and analytical style of a mathematically minded physician is professional and assertive for patients and unit staff. Unfortunately, there is a price to pay for assertive women (Williams 2016). What prompts the negative adjectives for highly effective women? Many powerful women describe the decrease in likeability as they rise in organizations.

MBA students at NYU read a fabricated Harvard Business School case about a very successful Silicon Valley entrepreneur named Howard or Heidi (McGinn 2000). Heidi was described by students as less kind and generous and more power hungry, manipulative, and assertive than Howard despite students looking at the exact same information for both gender names. In the Heidi/Howard case study, success and likeability are negatively correlated for women.

> "While she's really good at her job, she's just not as well liked by her peers." Raising gender bias in performance evaluations is met with thoughtful consideration of blind spots or anger and defensiveness. (Sandberg, *Lean In*)

> "Depend on no one to notice your worth. Being liked should not be your first priority." (Brzezinski, *Knowing Your Value: Women, Money, and Getting What You're Worth*)

Truth was evoked to improve processes. I felt no hunger for power. I declined leadership positions that were not good opportunities given the current staff dynamics and my limiting credentials in internal medicine, not emergency medicine. I had emotional intelligence, not risk aversion or low confidence. I believe in confidence building for all as discussed in the book by Kay and Shipman, *The Confidence Code: The Science and Art of Self-Assurance—What Women Should Know*. I planned to reside indefinitely in the community. Other individuals in leadership positions moved out of the community after their appointments. I was the best person to know my goals and how to achieve them.

The goals were excellent patient care, smooth operations, and staff retention. Over the course of six years, the sole mid-level provider position turned over every one to two years. Each provider asked me to advocate for them, which I did to no avail. Subsequent to my departure, the majority of the nursing staff, including the unit nursing leadership, departed. Efficient, quality patient care is associated with effective, experienced teams. I believed in the ICARE (Integrity, Compassion, Accountability, Respect, and Excellence), TEAMSTEPPS, and "ever better" teachings. I was supported by female chairpersons and a female observation unit director. I had been "leaning in" well before the book by Sheryl Sandberg *Lean In*, a birthday gift from my parents in 2013. Suddenly, with male leadership I experienced intense pushback. I carried a copy of an article reviewing this pushback to that pivotal meeting, and I had read Erin Callan Montella's *Full Circle: A Memoir of Leaning in Too Far and the Journey Back*. "I have struggled with my own story. I think many of us do. Even putting our experiences into a framework that has logical flow is difficult, but I now know why it is critical to try to know our stories."

> "Wisdom may be received or learned. Cherish those who make the time and energy to share it with others so their journey may be less painful. Live your values so there will be no regrets when each day is done and a lifetime of days are behind you. Reach for greater equality for all." (Dalai Lama)

I perceive myself as strong, well-intentioned, resilient, and capable. I never believed otherwise. There is not a confidence issue or risk aversion in me. I know my value. A nonjudgmental cultural check and reflection seem indicated.

The key lessons about power and control follow.

Power and Control

- Complaints are opportunities to dialogue and improve teamwork and work processes.
- Individuals who challenge leadership process and skills for the betterment of the work environment are not inappropriate.

- Reject leadership conclusions that lack all stakeholders' perspectives.
- Double standards exist with tribalism and biases.
- Tribalism and "pay to play" do not engender a sense of fairness.
- Good leadership respects and values all team members and their contributions.
- Good leadership listens to all voices and includes all members in shared decision making.
- Equal pay for equal work is just and fair.
- Transparency engenders better decision making and accountability

6

Abuse of Power and Control

The foundation of the conflict pyramid is the silencing voices of others and disrespect. This is manifested further with slights, discrediting statements, harassment, fear, bias, violence, and control. These maladaptive behaviors, as a continuum, lead to absence of a team, truth, safety, justice, peace, and power for the disadvantaged. At an extreme, these negative interactions are truly abusive. My personal experiences exemplify both positive and negative behaviors in the workforce, as would be expected in any large community. While our culture is recognizing more victimization in the work environment, the corollary by necessity requires the recognition of more perpetrators in the work environment. Accountability for these perpetrators and their enablers is a huge culture shift, especially when the prioritization of the bottom line of revenue and productivity allows enforcers to look the other way. People and morality need to be prioritized over money.

"You got to go along to get along." (Hillary Jordan, *Mudbound*). Unfortunately, to me this sounds like tolerate the status quo. And how do individuals who are excluded from sitting at the table "get along" when they are not even invited to the "game" or allowed to carry the ball? I sensed a definitive personal change in my professional standing when the leadership became male in my department. Normal issues were now a problem, attached with negativity directed at me. I had no voice and no physician team. As a result, I had no respect. I had effectively been kicked off the field and into the women's locker room. All game plans were discussed in the male locker room. Team allegiance was strong and in full display.

When I advocated for myself, defamatory actions arose. Some prior gender issues became more apparent. "Many women in the workforce … deal with unwanted advances and harassment the best we can" (Sandberg 2017). Studies demonstrate the failure of diversity programs (Dobbin 2016) and harassment training (see Appendix: Harassment Avoidance, page 109). Friendly colleagues would allude to negativity toward me espoused by the male administrators around the hospital at large, despite the fact that I continued to have no clinical performance issues and was well received in my unit. Off-service physicians approached me and alluded to efforts to collect negative comments about me, stating, "I didn't say anything," and expressing the administrator's disdain for me. "You two really don't get along." Interdepartmental operational issues and misunderstandings were possibly allowed and clearly not de-escalated, leading to a negative narrative termed non-collegial behavior—otherwise known as gaslighting to me. The language of performance evaluations became tainted with negative tones (Biernat 2012).

Defamatory actions included serial meetings by the hospitalist service (comprised of physicians who care for adult patients in the hospital setting only) over a period of years referring to me as a problem and collecting cases of hand-offs not meeting their satisfaction. To the contrary, my interpretation of the interactions involved a senior female physician expected to subordinate herself to junior faculty, most vocally male, on the hospitalist service.

Interpersonal conflict in this male structure was not a matter of misunderstanding that could be corrected with dialogue and information (see Appendix: Process and Communication for Action, page 101, which I provided to male leadership). The conflict was seeded in power and control, and harassment was used to maintain an entrenched patriarchy. Perceptions of managerial style were colored by gender bias and power (Wiley 1982). The similarity to the armed forces confronting gender discrimination in a large, entrenched institution seemed evident. I proffered a letter to make the evident issues as transparent as possible and to entreat the leadership to raise the bar on civil discourse in the work setting. I wanted my objection to this behavior to be clearly documented with my own paper trail. Legal advocates will want documentation that the appropriate leadership was informed of the inappropriate behavior in real time. I did not recreate history as legal pundits often do to control a narrative.

> September 2016
> Dear_____,
>   It has come to my attention during this review that
> I have been publicly ostracized in hospitalist meetings.
> "She is a known problem. She has been discussed mul-
> tiple times in our meetings because of these problems."
> This practice is not in keeping with the hospital mission
> to respect all employees and work toward teamwork. I
> perceive this as character defamation and harassment.
> I request you educate the hospitalist service to refrain
> from bashing individuals and encourage them to dis-
> cuss process and communication styles.

Efforts of mine to advocate for unit staff members with my senior position and understanding of group dynamics should have been believable and actionable. This is the injustice of male patriarchy: to not believe women. In retrospect, these e-mails, along with other faculty e-mails, were presumably searched by the legal department and shared with the department leadership for evidence to remove unwanted faculty. The apparent glitch to this seemingly standard university process was that my e-mails were transparent and professional, and they included efforts to improve patient care and hospital processes. These possible internal searches made some male administrators look ineffectual, and they probably knew it. There was a clear mantra to the emergency administration that negative interactions were not to appear in e-mail diatribes, which could potentially create liabilities for the university. One administrator repeatedly projected his issues verbally because he would be unlikely to maintain appropriate talking points in an e-mail. This sounds like some individuals who sidetrack into scary discussions on Twitter rants. To protect me, one former co-author and male administrator even warned me to not write e-mails in anger because these lapses might be used as cause for dismissal. I was not prone to the ranting that I witnessed from other faculty. Any potential future discovery, if university legal proceedings resulted, would include my appropriate and professional e-mails and paper records.

Women in the unit were devalued and belittled. Nurses were also left out of information loops. Metrics were ignored if the male leadership did not shine. Aggregate data minimized the role of women and were attributed to male leaders if laudable (Ruiz 2016). According to male administrators, the nurses presumably liked me and my style more than other providers because "she is a woman," and "of course women have better patient satisfaction" (Choo 2017). I felt diminished by a male administrator. Equality in education and training years disappear in the workforce when status, power, and money are in play.

My contributions and ideas were hidden with compiled data and devalued. A pattern of power and control dynamics was utilized by the male leadership. These dynamics are easily recognizable as an expert in partner violence. The behaviors are the same whether in the home or the workplace. Intimidation and verbal threats of dismissal were conveyed to me with an administrative witness. As a physician at the height of my career with numerous accolades and exemplary work, I felt dumbfounded at the true lack of communication and leadership skills I witnessed.

Undermining, attacking team dynamics and military styles were projected by defensive, less capable men. The male perspective of my work ethic included malicious intent, negative attributes, and an undermining nature. This misrepresentation embodied a false conspiracy theory against me. Animosity arose from male leadership. I even explained in the pivotal meeting that the male leadership had no complaints initiated by me at any point during my six-year position. All of my comments were positive process and skill set suggestions, or responses to other individuals' complaints in an attempt to de-escalate conflict and team build. Unfortunately, I was not on the team. I experienced more limited communication and few meetings.

I believed that as an established and respected senior physician, I could advocate for patients, staff, and my unit to improve operations. Unfortunately, misrepresentation by leadership made this impossible. Male leadership missed or willfully ignored the premise that bright, capable, and well-intentioned individuals were not problems. Therefore all unit issues were, in fact, process issues that could be discussed and resolved to improve unit operations. Dialogue, explanations for common understanding, and respect were elements of positive team interactions. Negative presumptions, excuse labeling, and blaming lacked of elements of teamwork and respect. No personal blame needed to be assigned to any individual. Resolved issues needed not be placed in paper trails for administrative leverage and control.

Female leaders are often described as nasty and difficult women. Often women are visionaries, activists, and agents of change. Our likability will be questioned, and our behaviors will seem unacceptable. Assertive women are described differently in performance reviews (Snyder 2014). The insidious negativity attributed to powerful assertive women is well documented. In my case, the clear misrepresentation is a common accusation that is believable for a paper trail to protect less capable and insecure men. The "overly pushy woman syndrome" is also an attack falsely projected by vulnerable men who feel threatened, similar to a sexual assault perpetrator saying the sex was consensual. These are the standard talking points. "Clearly, women who are assertive suffer a backlash" notes Brzezinski in her book, *Knowing Your Value: Women, Money, and Getting What You're Worth*.

The double standard is monumental. Over three decades, I have been aware of male promiscuity, substance abuse, vulgarity, and anger—which are met by compassionate administrators with remediation and tolerance. Most of these individuals still have faculty appointments. I had relentlessly advocated for patients and staff and was labeled noncollegial.

I did not subordinate myself to the wishes of others when it was improper for patient care or placed me as a handmaid with disrespect to my position, experience, and expertise. I value fairness and equality in the workforce. Operational issues arose when I exerted my experience and judgment for the benefit of patients. I did not allow less senior off-service physicians to subordinate me with their work redistribution attempts. I was not the handmaid of youthful men outside my unit, the most outspoken of whom were comparable in age to my children and stepchildren. I believe these more youthful physicians, some possibly more insecure in their skill sets, were emboldened, even encouraged by their director. This director appeared to be seeking criticism to put me in my place as an outspoken advocate for patients and staff. (Of note, this director was no longer in his leadership position within a year of my grievance and EEOC filings.) This bottom line created disruption and irked medical administrators, even though I was their clinical peer and objectively outperformed them. There is still not the time, energy, or interest at some large institutions to see the flaws and implicit bias in the selection of some staff for the decider's self-interest and not university, department, or unit mission. Diverse decision-making bodies are more just and seek the common good for employees and patients. The whole concept of patient dumping from my unit to the hospital was emblematic of the confirmation bias and lack of knowledge the leadership had of my ability. When comparing abilities, sometimes individuals who are not in your radar are ahead, not behind. Was the university mantra "ever better" just for male employees? "It's time to slam the door shut on that era. And to open another door, through which we can welcome equality: between genders, among marital partners, for everyone in every circumstance" states Solnit in her book, *Men Explain Things to Me*.

I had been treated more respectfully in elementary school than in my most recent physician position. I had never been reprimanded in a disciplinary fashion in my entire life. Clearly, issues were discussed as they arose, but my best intentions were always acknowledged, and reasonable steps forward were always mutually attained. I had been the model student and employee with large amounts of independence my entire life, due to my high work ethic and performance standards. I always complied with directives.

The male leadership utilized a pattern of power and control dynamics. These dynamics are easily recognizable as an expert in partner violence. The behaviors are the same whether in the home or the workplace. My experiences included male leaders standing over me and yelling at me, "You are on the edge." This was perceived as a threat to my employment after I had offered to assist a struggling colleague with my administrative skill set in exchange for appropriate recognition and remuneration. Arizona State University found that angry men gain influence whereas angry women lose influence. Additional experiences included mocking me ("You think you are good at communication. You are not."), baiting and goading me to say I felt unhappy ("If you are unhappy, you could leave. You can leave this job if you don't like it.") Male leadership solicited complaints about other staff which I did not offer. They talked down to me as a subordinate, although I was a clinical equal and was even senior to youthful physicians. I stated on more than one occasion that I was treated as less than and was serially slighted compared to my male clinical colleagues. These actions preserved the social order status quo.

> "The reason most often given for women leaving a position was lack of engagement or enjoyment in the job." (Turner 2012)

> "Find what it is that makes you feel invincible and in control ... We live in a bully culture." (Bennett 2016)

Silicon Valley female employees shared many suboptimal experiences: feeling shamed and less than; feeling disrespected and as though their accomplishments didn't matter; sensing they were not in a position to speak up; and experiencing no accountability and no one to speak with about concerns. These women wanted to continue to work. (Benner 2017)

> Still the percentage of women at the top of corporations has significantly trailed behind participation levels in the workforce. (Lang 2004)

Win-lose

The male leaders did not appear to support individual employees who were not on the leadership team but focused on the interests of others external to their units to be an administrative team member for hospital leadership. This leadership did not perceive win-win interactions and appeared to seek the weak individual to take the blame for process issues. When I suggested process improvement, this was reframed unnecessarily as a loss or reprimand for someone else. This structure resulted in animosity between employees and a need to remove the agent of change/improvement who was perceived as an antagonist and a problem. Mismatch of objective and subjective data is misrepresentation. Misrepresentation as a problem is defamatory not dissimilar to President Trump calling Rep. Maxine Waters "low IQ" or Senator Elizabeth Warren "Pocahontas." My experiences are representative of tribalism and otherism at its worst. I do not believe most work environments or men in the workforce devolve to this level. I share my experiences hoping they are an extreme, but I wish to broaden the scope of understanding the snowball effect of misguided narratives without dialogue and true efforts to stand in another's shoes.

The male leadership team supported each other's agendas, padded each other's paper trails, and created their win-win and tit-for-tat scenarios. On one occasion, an administrator actually deleted an e-mail supportive of me when it may have conflicted with the negative paper trail in motion. Amusingly, every encounter with me appeared to have a predetermined, prepared end point before my input. These same male leaders were surprised and annoyed that I had valid points and different perspectives. In most cases, as the senior, more experienced physician, I advocated for the patient. The less experienced physician or the referring physician, who was less knowledgeable about my unit's standard of care, was annoyed that I redirected care on the patient's behalf. I repeatedly tried to address issues proactively and in a rational manner for team building, problem solving, and conflict resolution, but the irrational, reactive leadership team (no room for players on the captain's team) continued to cast blame on me. I was labeled noncollegial for having a different perspective. Patient care was my primary concern, whereas others argued over workload distribution and interdepartmental turf battles. Several attempts were made for me to register guilt and apologize in order to continue the negative narrative for my potential dismissal. I appeared obstinate in their eyes and always had to be right. Did these male leaders think I was blind to their narrative?

Confirmation bias echoed in the hospital because there were no routine interactions for team building (see Appendix: Recognition of Errors to Find Opportunities, page 105). Only conflict was discussed, making this implicit bias understandable. Information gaps and low transparency abounded. Even the pivotal meeting demonstrated premature closure of a discussion, affective errors based on negative emotions, and anchoring of a false idea. Any employee effort to respectfully disagree as an agent of change, improvement, and progress was more data that the employee was not receptive to leadership feedback. This false sense of winners and losers resulted because all stakeholders were not perceived by leadership to be on the same team.

This confirmation bias was readily apparent when an administrator with whom I rarely interacted belittled my ability to count work hours and shifts—a skill I attained in high school waitressing. She clearly had no idea of my summa cum laude mathematics degree, extensive leadership and research accomplishments. This same administrator was apparently unwilling or unable to connect the dots when I was inappropriately reprimanded harshly for missing a meeting about which the male leadership had "forgotten" to inform me.

The emergency department (ED) interacts with every department. Historically, the ED has been discredited as a lesser specialty. Only one medical school classmate of mine entered this specialty and practiced in the air force. Even my father, a retired orthopedic surgeon, was initially disappointed when I embraced this specialty after training in internal medicine. The ED performed contortions at the request of the hospital leadership to please every inpatient service. There are limits to appropriate expectations and reasonable patient hand-offs. Each department may create processes for their own department, and at any complexity. Similar to individuals, departments may control only their own actions and not those of others. Issues that arise may then be addressed by the department that actually created, controlled and implemented the policies. No department or individual should be the handmaid to another. I read Margaret Atwood's *The Handmaid's Tale* in the 1980s after a first edition was gifted to me by my mother-in-law. She was an extremely bright and capable woman who graduated with a major in chemistry. She, like my own mother, was resigned to being a housewife and mother by societal norms. She expressed her joy for my ambitions and career. Misunderstandings happen when there is poor communication.

Most individuals are aware of the information explosion in society and the electronic medical record. As a problem solver and math major, I never prided myself in memorizing large volumes of information. As a physician in a high-volume, rapid-turnover unit, I would access patient information as needed, committing only essential information to memory, a few key facts. My goal was to get the right care to people at the right time. Upon transfer to another service, receiving providers would be referred to the electronic record for patient information I had not committed to memory. This inconvenient truth was somehow infuriating to one service, seemingly fueled by nontransparent venting and emergency department bashing for years. There was no lapse in quality patient care. There was no need for a senior physician on one service to subordinate herself to another service by reading the chart over the phone to a provider who had electronic access to this information. The nurses at this same hospital efficiently sent a written report and were available for questions as needed. What prevented a simple explanation of style and information accessibility?

Why did conflict have to be escalated and not de-escalated? Defamation of character in serial meetings over years seemed quite inappropriate. But this was not simply defamation of my career as a physician. This was defamation of me as a person and everything for which my life was intended to represent, including advocacy for others, improved communication, and team building. What noncollegial behavior? This term was being used as a twisted, catch-all phrase for a predetermined goal of my potential dismissal.

> "St. Augustine once said that the definition of a nation was a multitude of rational beings united by the common objects of their love. And the great thing about the American experiment is that what we have loved in common is the idea of fair play. The best way we guarantee fair play for me is to guarantee fair play for you." (Jon Meacham, Random House Executive Editor)

The key lessons about abuse of power and control follow.

Abuse of Power and Control

- Silencing voices of team members is a form of disrespect.
- False narratives are a form of harassment and defamation.
- Bias, discrimination, and control of team members sometimes includes abusive behaviors.
- Individuals should not be held accountable for confusion and complaints precipitated by poor leadership styles and communication.
- Checks and balances on all positions need to be in place, especially for small units where decisions may be made for leadership's self-interest.

2017 Women's March

Men of Quality
Do Not Fear
Equality

Afterword

An affiliation with the university for thirty-five years was terminated. As you have seen in numerous illustrations in previous chapters, I was subjected to a litany of gender bias, discrimination, and unprofessional treatment in my workplace. A prior e-mail to the associate medical director had stated my interest in dedicating the next ten years of my career to this community hospital. I had repeatedly requested additional responsibilities to my emergency medical administrators. I had applied for alternate positions to increase my visibility and to team build. Just two years earlier, I was deemed a strong candidate for the highest physician position at this community hospital. I donated money to the university and belonged to the affiliated philanthropic organization.

Did I have to advertise more verbosely my connections and dedication to the university? For the most part, I have lived a relatively privileged life. My father completed medical school and an orthopedic residency at this university. He practiced in this community his entire career, supervising university residents and students. My brother completed an MBA at the university. My three children all attended the university. Of my three children, one successfully transitioned to a surgical residency, one became a high school math teacher, and the other became a language specialist in the army. Who thought I wasn't trying to fit in? Who wouldn't let me fit in? Did I naively believe university faculty were actually evaluated on objective merits of their work? Where was the fairness of a true meritocracy?

Paradoxes appear in organizations. When companies adopt a more merit-based compensation system, they actually become more gender biased (Castilla 2010). Meritocracy has been refuted in Silicon Valley (Chang 2018; Kantor 2014). Constructed criteria have redefined merit to justify discrimination (Uhlmann 2005). The male culture creates a false choice between a perceived functional male team and a disruptive woman. The true choice is an inclusive, improved culture with policies and procedures to address harassment and discrimination. It is unfortunate that some individuals feel vulnerable and need to exclude others' voices and participation in order to maintain power and control.

> Reflect 15 minutes each day:
> 5 minutes on your dreams and desires
> 5 minutes on others
> 5 minutes on the reality that each individual shares the same dreams and desires
> (Dalai Lama)

> "Be kind, for everyone you meet is fighting a battle you know nothing about." (Wendy Mass, *The Candymakers*)

A pattern of minimization and marginalization was evident to me for years. Power and control dynamics in the workforce may be more apparent to individuals like me who have more knowledge of these dynamics. Similar to partner violence in the community, perpetrators of unjust power and control behaviors may be a small percentage of an institution, but they can have large effects with significant staff disillusionment, turnover, and lost productivity. Lack of equity and diversity will not ultimately be cost neutral or productive.

Transferring from a university hospital, where cutting-edge ideas were sought, to a community hospital, where the mere completion of clinical shifts was desired, was clearly not an expectation of mine. I felt like an inconsequential pawn in a male-dominated chess league. I spent the end of my career in a position that was quite effortless for me with appropriate preparation. Lower acuity was replaced with higher volume that fit perfectly with my efficient skill set and quick, problem-solving nature. I had survived academia with three young children, a divorce, and social tumult. I now experienced a stable relationship, an empty nest, and a less taxing clinical position with no academic responsibilities. I love change and had new responsibilities every three to five years for my entire career. This joy is an extension of my love of problem solving. My love of change may be one reason I unnerve other staff who do not have the same proclivity. I had known I could continue in this position for many years with no possibility that my ability would be inadequate with the current leadership. I had settled into the routine. I had believed my glory years would simply be less glorious.

It's so sad that some staff can't find some means to structure their day to work for themselves without imposing on others. No system works for everyone, and everyone is unique—thus the confusion, complaints, and operational challenges. One of my closest confidants was a middle-aged African American woman who was a medical technician in our unit. She too witnessed the disrespect and double standard toward me as a senior female attending physician. She too experienced the treatment as less than and being serially slighted. She remarked to me in a text after my dismissal, "Hi Dr. ... I'm so heartbroken. ____ _ gave me your number. I hope that was okay. Thank you for talking to me. Most doctors overlook the PCT [Patient Care Technician], but you did not. Will it be okay if we stay in touch?" Her loss this year to a massive stroke still reverberates. Thankfully, she was able to return to her home state and be with family prior to this tragic event.

Team building around common interests had been enjoyable and beneficial to cohesion and ultimately patient care as might be suggested by Carnegie in his book, *How to Win Friends and Influence People.* Activities included providing bulbs for another's garden; starting a Powerball pool to hear everyone's dreams learning the names of children, grandchildren, and pets; exploring relationships that eventually led to marriages and children; and filling in gaps for personal losses with incidental gifts of food and gift shop trinkets. My husband prepared a turkey dinner for several years, which became a ritual for Thanksgiving. After traveling out of town for family holidays, I would return with a container of a favorite dish from a son's restaurant that one nurse discovered on an outing with her significant other. Sharing stories of spouses serving in the fire department or police department when community events were in the news was not uncommon. Several staff significant others and family members visiting the unit thanked me for easing the rigor of a tumultuous working environment and making work shifts more enjoyable for their loved ones.

Wisdom comes from hearing all perspectives and advocating for patients before staff. The process of conflict resolution and team building requires a seat at the table and a voice for all. There is still evidence of speaking about others without their presence at the table. Unconscious biases exist but can be tempered by diversity on all decision-making bodies. The mere presence of diverse teams at the table will hold many administrative bodies accountable. One example is the 2018 cancellation of the Roseanne Barr's role in a sitcom after a racist tweet. Basics of childhood golden rules and mutual respect go a long way. Partner violence advocates have an event to "walk in her shoes" each year that highlights the need to be open to another's situation. Insanity is doing the same thing over and over and expecting a different outcome. Change is empowering. Resources exist to engage men to be agents of change in gender initiatives (Prime 2009).

> "You never really understand a person until you consider things from his point of view until you climb into his skin and walk around in it." (Harper Lee, *To Kill a Mockingbird*)

I would add "her point of view." I felt essentially blacklisted from any emergency medicine position in the community. My spouse is independently employed in the community. My parents; some of my siblings, children, and grandchildren; and my lifelong home are in the community. I feel connected to this community. I could have been a poster child for loving my state and community. I had no intention of living elsewhere.

"Women have been described as rooted in communities, often more than men, and therefore can bring about change more effectively." (Leymah Roberta Gbowee, a Liberian peace activist)

Male leadership did not wish to incorporate my voice, skill set, or energy in the workforce at the community or university hospitals. This type of incident may only happen in some departments and some institutions, but significant casualties occur nonetheless. The mentors for the upcoming generations will still have the old institutional appearance, lacking the diversity so desperately needed in some departments. The pipeline and pathways for women in medicine to achieve leadership will continue to be followed (Lautenberger 2014). "The goddess Athena is a powerful image of a fierce warrior with a full range of qualities including character, wisdom, courage and promise for all women" as noted by Johnson in the book *Athena Rising: How and Why Men Should Mentor Women*.

Legalities Abound

Legal concepts including collusion become relevant. Collusion is the knowing or unknowing coordination of activities. Motivation also is pertinent. Motivation usually comprises several common aspirations: money, ideology, coercion, and ego (MICE). Legal authorities counsel that it is difficult to determine malicious intent or incompetence with a nuanced series of interactions for years. The activities, although awful, may be lawful. *Severe* or *pervasive* is a high bar for unlawful behavior. Maybe institutions need change to address flaws in current employment policies and procedures that permit contrived paper trails and dismissals. An organization can always put something in its human resource file.

"Never attribute to malice that which can be adequately explained by stupidity, but don't rule out malice." (Heinlein 1941)

"We should honor—not attack—those who have stood up for equality and other cherished American values." (Intel CEO Brian Krzanich, August 16, 2017)

"Will continue to focus my efforts on inspiring every person that they can do anything through the power of sport which promotes ... unity, diversity, and inclusion." (Under Armour CEO Kevin Plank, August 14, 2017)

"Now is the time to understand more, so that we may fear less." (Thomas Friedman, *Thank You for Being Late: An Optimist's Guide to Thriving in the Age of Accelerations*)

The contrived paper trail includes overarching verbiage that is simply not credible: "poor work ethic," "sees only her perspective," "lack of accountability," "noncollegial," and "unprovoked attack." This violent reference is particularly offensive with my lifetime of nonviolence advocacy (see Appendix: Beyond Credible Alternative Facts—My Story, page 107). The series of complaints previously reviewed at the time of their initial discussion with leadership should be perceived as normal issues in a busy emergency department with a new unit. Complaints could be routinely managed by leadership after brief discussion with the employee and review of all pertinent perspectives. However, these issues reappeared in a paper trail. Contrary to any effective process, it was clear that the purpose of the formal interactions was to create a paper trail to remove an employee with a superior skill set who attempted to be an exemplary employee and advance her career. Balanced information and feedback were rarely provided. This reconstruction exercise is to improve understanding for other employees and their future interactions.

"To carry on in the spring of 2017 as if what was happening was anything approaching normalcy required a

determined suspension of critical faculties and tremen-
dous powers of denial." (Senator Jeff Flake, *Conscience
of a Conservative*)

Some of the medical administrators that passed judgment never
even met with me over issues until this consequential meeting. As issues were brought to my attention, explanatory and clarifying e-mails
were sent in real time to appropriate administrators up the power structure, but my experience was that these issues were not to be discussed
openly for fear of opening Pandora's box. Administrators preferred
to handle issues behind the scenes with the possible hope they would
correct themselves. Did these individuals even know my career and
life of excelling beyond my peers, expertise in communication, power
and control dynamics, and a core value for nonviolence with Gandhi
as a role model?

"You start at your most popular and least capable. You
end at your most capable and least popular. And it is a
privilege." (Tony Blair, former prime minister of Great
Britain)

"Always remember others may hate you but those who
hate you don't win unless you hate them. And then you
destroy yourself." (Richard M. Nixon, thirty-seventh
US president, in his White House farewell address)

"Dissent is as American as apple pie." (Dan Rather,
former CBS News anchor)

False Narratives

Many accusations appear to be projections of common causes for dismissal of prior employees with a male perspective. The common sce-
nario would be "it just isn't a good fit." A good fit for whom? The unit

ran like a finely tuned machine when I staffed the unit. The staff appreciated me. This less secure administrator even made note of searching for the "mole," as if in an espionage novel. I felt this administrator was not comfortable with competent people around him. Research shows men feel insecure when female partners succeed (Marcotte 2013). I would surmise colleagues feel similarly when women excel. Employers also cite the consideration of "cultural fit" as a top priority for employee happiness, productivity, and retention (Rivera 2015). Knowingly or not, maintenance of the status quo, misogyny and all, was chosen over clinical excellence and equity in the workforce. My vacated position was filled with a less accomplished male peer with similar credentialing.

> "No one with self-respect wants to work in a place where the boss not only won't back you up when the going gets tough, but will turn on you with a vengeance-especially when there's a need to divert attention from his own shortcomings." (McCarthy 2017)

My unit metrics and patient satisfaction were superior. As in the arts, performance is everything. Or not, for some. For many universities that laud big data, the cherry-picking of rare, subjective operational discrepancies in a high-volume, short-stay unit is ludicrous or intentional. This felt like President Trump, a vulnerable individual in a new leadership position, firing intelligence staff and cabinet members, many of whom were career employees with integrity and staff support.

The pivotal and volatile meeting was subsequently described as a "counseling session" in response to my grievance. This description is laughable because I orchestrated the meeting, apparently to the dismay of those in attendance. This once again demonstrated premeditated judgment against me with no input of my perspective. Presumptive premeditation by male leadership and revelation of the true intent to dismiss me shortly afterward was apparent. Alternatively, renaming this meeting a counseling session from a general discussion was to illustrate appropriate processes for addressing employee "deficiencies" clearly lacking in their contrived paper trail. This appeared similar to law enforcement planting evidence. I was denied a team and a voice, even in the pivotal meeting described.

> "My hope is to help those whose voices should also be heard." (Taylor Swift, advocating for victims of sexual assault)

None of my years of service and excellence could overcome the apparent negative narrative of male leaders and the defamation created by serial, nontransparent gatherings over six or more years. Little to no effort was made by leadership at this community hospital to include me in operational activities despite my stellar performance. Subjective negativity by male leaders was exaggerated and repeated to the unquestioning belief of those in the line of command. No verification or clarification by interaction with me was pursued. Institutional logic would lead one to believe surely seven or more male medical administrators with the same information would have to be correct in ousting the disruptive senior female physician—me.

Gender bias and confirmation bias were unchecked. Similar to the plot in Agatha Christie's *Murder on the Orient Express*, no one individual needed to take responsibility for the bad deed of murdering one evil individual who had a negative ripple effect on them all. Some male individuals discredit strong women because they can. They are not held accountable by their male team—not dissimilar to male sexual predators and perpetrators of partner violence. History repeats itself. Bad behavior will continue if perpetrators are not held accountable. Meanwhile, many women are the casualties. The male administrative culture is not adequately responding to all employee complaints and needs. Diverse oversight committees should be instituted to improve transparency and hold all administrators accountable. The problem, addressed by the Women's Media Center, continues to be limited representation and visibility of women and minorities. "Men need to break the 'man code' which reinforces the male culture, keeping the company of other men, primarily engaging in male activities and turning a blind eye on bad behavior" (Halter 2015).

Early retirement has its consequences. There is less time to make retirement contributions, less time for principal growth with earlier fund withdrawal, more expensive annuities to cover more years of retirement, and lower monthly security benefits. Most would understand that early retirement alters the household of the affected individual. Middle-class households are being squeezed with limited maternity leave and family leave, as well as a lack of affordable childcare and healthcare (Quart 2018). My children were baffled and irked by my thrifty style during their college years with my seemingly solid career as a physician with the same university for decades. I protected them for the most part from the insecurity of potential job loss. I knew women earned less over the duration of their lifetimes and statistically lived longer. I prepared accordingly, even more so over the last eight years of my career. I could not prevent the inevitable desire of the male leadership to remove me from my position despite proactive self-advocacy. The grievance process and human resources appear structured to benefit the institution. The Equal Employment Opportunity Commission (EEOC), possibly overwhelmed with raised 2017 voices, may be unsuited to address cultural shifts and more nuanced systemic issues of institutions. No further negativity was desired on my part. I would ponder the Buddha phrase, *"I do not accept your gift."* What's more, "Buddhify offers a fun, game-ified approach to creating a meditation practice" according to Huffington in her book, *Thrive.*

But I still wanted the voice that I had been repeatedly denied. I was unwilling to sign any potential future nondisclosure agreement or confidentiality agreement if there was a successful legal proceeding. Any legal case would languish for years and incur excessive amounts of money that I could not jeopardize, especially with an early retirement. I was also informed any potential settlement would be relatively small. Transparent institutions that espouse morality and accountability should not need NDAs. Voices are being raised for culture change. Legal action against institutions, advocacy books, transparency through journalism and women's marches will draw attention to academic and work environments that do not treat all students and employees morally and fairly. Unwritten rules have allowed inappropriate and immoral behavior. It is time to accept this inconvenient truth and change. Resolute action for change and equity are necessary. Society must listen to and believe women's stories. Women and men of quality need to stand together against a continued assault on equality in the workplace. Women's suffrage was not enough. We must continue to stand for our rights and those of other disadvantaged populations because we have not yet achieved equity and full empowerment.

The double standard for women advocating for their career advancement is well documented. Passionately advocating for patients and unit staff would be normal male behavior described as physician excellence and used for university promotion, career advancement, and university pride. The male leadership demonstrated gender bias when they applied negative attributes to me for drawing recognition to my accomplishments and ideas for improvement. I had a voice to share, and I have a voice today.

Many positive experiences occurred over thirty-four years of university interactions. However, the self-serving actions of some male leadership, possibly attributable to gender bias, need to be corrected so all work environments can be viewed in the positive light of the core values and ideals of the institution. Some universities need to revise their policies and procedures around harassment, defamation, and retaliation because its current policies are seemingly inadequate. There are elements of clear denial and inaction toward credible issues brought to leadership's attention. Shared decision making and transparency are woefully lacking. Amended policies need to be more prohibitive of immoral but lawful behavior, as is the case at many other universities. Amended policies need to be more supportive of women and disadvantaged populations. Currently, the bar for acceptable behavior is too low.

My experiences add additional context to recent criticism of some universities over the administrative approach to alleged harassment and misconduct. These universities repeatedly fail to intervene against retaliation when issues are brought to leadership's attention. Divisive environments should not be attributed to those employees who draw attention to existing harassment and misconduct but to the perpetrators and the poor judgment, unresponsiveness, or inaction of university officials. Blacklisting and future negative references are known consequences for those attempting to address misconduct. Subsequent institutional corrective action to address misconduct never repairs the careers of the whistle-blowers. Some universities have a history of protecting perpetrators and ignoring victims' pleas for help. The institution fails to protect students and employees from retaliation.

The similarity of the stories and responses from the administration when issues are raised is clear. This pattern of behavior, including denials of wrongdoing despite immorality and inappropriate actions, and the minimization with universities spending millions of dollars for reports and legal cases are reminiscent of Penn State, Jerry Sandusky, Joe Paterno, and repetitive acts of pedophilia in academia. The more recent case of Dr. Larry Nassar at Michigan State University and the Olympic gymnastics training camp also exists as an example. Even the most honorable professions, the priesthood and medicine, have bad actors. Power corrupts some individuals. The denials, reframing of issues, and contrived narratives against informants are worse on the reputations of the universities than proactively addressing known incidents and issues to find solutions and actions to improve the environment for all. Universities must address the underlying culture of gender inequality in academia. Some universities are stepping up in the best interest of these universities to apologize to all women, as did the dean of Harvard's Business School in the *Huffington Post*.

Universities and administrations need to be held responsible for the low bar for morality and the breadth of immoral behavior that is accepted in academia. Some administrators do not demonstrate the moral authority to lead. Institutions of higher learning should be setting a high bar for the moral fabric of society. Students and employees who seek opportunities to raise behavior standards and increase equity and morality on campus are not attacking universities, but they are partnering with administrators and employees who are unaware due to ignorance or unconscious bias (Giang 2015; Lublin 2014) or are disregarding the flaws in the current environment. Universities and administrations must be held accountable for retaliation against employees and friends of the university who seek only to contribute to the betterment of the university as designed by their ideals. Women who raise concerns about morality and equity in the workplace should not be compromised and lose career potential for patriarchal maintenance of the status quo. Men and their careers should not be protected to an extreme despite verifiable issues with equity and morality. These injustices should not be perpetuated by leadership's inaction to raise the bar for acceptable behaviors. Clearly, investigational and legal departments that are structured for the defense of current university policies must be redesigned to allow improvement of processes for greater equity and higher morality to be embraced and not shunned.

> "The arc of the moral universe is long, but it bends towards justice." (Theodore Parker, nineteenth-century abolitionist and Unitarian minister)

Many institutions still exude, "Put up or get out." One more woman proudly refused to put up, transparently documented her concerns about equity and morality in the workforce, and has been forced out. Early retirement began for me at the age of fifty-seven. I recall a perspective of my youngest daughter when she was in preschool and I was in my midthirties. She inquired about my age, to which I dutifully responded. She incredulously asked, "Is that a number?" Currently, I am a middle-aged baby boomer still full of hope, joy, and energy. Thus ended a career but not a well-lived life. As a high-energy, articulate advocate for women and the disadvantaged, I hope to continue my lifelong values. Hopefully, future generations will have fewer lemons in life but possibly more opportunities for lemonade. I am where I belong. I am turning the page and ending only several chapters included in this partial memoir. I am thrilled to see two of our six children married this year. I pray for more grandchildren in the not-too-distant future. I am traveling with my spouse on a two-week vacation to exalt in the time with which I have been blessed. Life will be wonderful. A peak experience of life—a well-deserved retirement after a dedicated career—is claimed. I feel conflicted about my current relationship with the university, having experienced the best of times and the worst as well. Michelle Obama reminds us, "When they go low, we go high."

> 8-8-17
> Dear ___,
>
> I intend to retire from the university on September 8, 2017.
>
> I will remember my thirty-five years associated with the university as a student, resident, and faculty member. I enjoyed the many clinical, research, and teaching opportunities I was provided for a fulfilling academic career at this institution.
>
> Sincerely,
> Pandora B. Angel, MD

> "You are allowed to be disappointed when it feels like life's benched you. What you aren't allowed to do is miss your opportunity to lead from the bench." (Abby Wambach, Barnard College commencement, 2018)

I announce the passing, or possible sharing, of the baton as you finish this book. Your turn may have arrived. Act today to foster change for women in the workplace. We need constitutional recognition of equal rights for women, as stated by Supreme Court Justice Ruth Bader Ginsburg. Raise your voice to empower all individuals. Strive for equity. Do your part. Together we can change the world and the arc of the moral universe.

Call to Action

- Own your identity (via social media and organizational networks).
- Label yourself so others will not choose a false label for you.
- Write your own story. Choose. Seek validity from within.
- Do not speak for others because you may misrepresent them. State only your opinions.
- Have empathy for those who need to tear others down in order to succeed.
- Be grateful that you have the strength and ability to see the good beyond the injustice in the world.
- Remember it is always better to give than receive. Pay it forward with acts of kindness.
- Internalize your values. Think globally but act locally.
- Sacrifice for something bigger than yourself.
- Every day can be better than the previous day.
- There is no shame in living and trying your best.
- You only have control over your own actions, not others.
- Embrace the positive. Reject the negative. Live in the moment.
- Likeability is not the ultimate goal. Equality is the goal.
- Be the change in the world you want to see.
- Find luck and creativity in your own ideas.
- Success is achievable with appropriate goals.
- Personal best means success with no regrets.
- Accept fallibility.
- Embrace survivorship. "That which does not kill you makes you stronger."
- Advocate for others to achieve equality, diversity, tolerance, non-violence, and survivorship.

Action Pyramid
Pandora B. Angel, MD

Empowerment

Shared decision making

Fairness-Equity

Tolerance-Empathy

Amplify All Contributions

Inclusion-Teamwork

Listen to All Voices- Respect

Conflict Pyramid
Pandora B. Angel, MD

Control- No Power

Violence- No Peace

Bias -No Justice

Harassment, Fear -
No Safety

Discredit- No Truth

Slight- No Team

Silence- No Voice- No Respect

Domestic Abuse Intervention Programs
202 East Superior Street
Duluth, MN 66802
218-722-2781

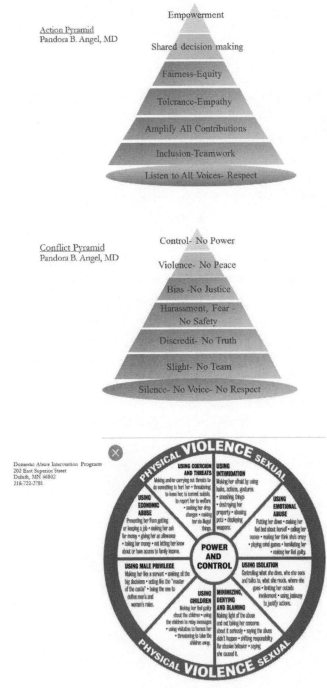

POWER AND CONTROL

PHYSICAL VIOLENCE SEXUAL

USING COERCION AND THREATS
Making and/or carrying out threats to do something to hurt her • threatening to leave her, to commit suicide, to report her to welfare • making her drop charges • making her do illegal things.

USING INTIMIDATION
Making her afraid by using looks, actions, gestures. • smashing things • destroying her property • abusing pets • displaying weapons.

USING ECONOMIC ABUSE
Preventing her from getting or keeping a job • making her ask for money • giving her an allowance • taking her money • not letting her know about or have access to family income.

USING EMOTIONAL ABUSE
Putting her down • making her feel bad about herself • calling her names • making her think she's crazy • playing mind games • humiliating her • making her feel guilty.

USING MALE PRIVILEGE
Making her like a servant • making all the big decisions • acting like the "master of the castle" • being the one to define men's and women's roles.

USING ISOLATION
Controlling what she does, who she sees and talks to, what she reads, where she goes • limiting her outside involvement • using jealousy to justify actions.

USING CHILDREN
Making her feel guilty about the children • using the children to relay messages • using visitation to harass her • threatening to take the children away.

MINIMIZING, DENYING AND BLAMING
Making light of the abuse and not taking her concerns about it seriously • saying the abuse didn't happen • shifting responsibility for abusive behavior • saying she caused it.

PHYSICAL VIOLENCE SEXUAL

Appendices

Inspirational Ideas for Hope

"Wisdom may be received or learned. Cherish those who make the time and energy to share it with others so their journey may be less painful. Live your values so there will be no regrets when each day is done and a lifetime of days are behind you. Reach for greater equality for all."

—Dalai Lama

"Complaining not allowed. Whiners may lose their sense of humor and ability to solve problems. So, stop complaining and act to make your life better."

—Pope Francis's sign at his Vatican residence

"Courage—judgment—integrity—dedication—these are the historic qualities … which, with God's help … will characterize our Government's conduct in the 4 stormy years that lie ahead."

—President-elect John F. Kennedy, address to the Massachusetts legislature, January 9, 1961

"Never give up. Never become bitter. Be hopeful. Be optimistic and Keep pushing."

—John Lewis, January 16, 2017

"We must always take sides. Neutrality helps the oppressor, never the victim. Silence encourages the tormentor, never the tormented."

—Elie Wiesel, *The Night Trilogy:*
Night, Dawn, the Accident

"Speaking truth to power means believing deeply in what you say and fighting every day to have that heard. It may not be popular; it means taking a risk, it means standing for something."

— Civil rights leader Bayard Rustin,
Huffington Post, December 22, 2015

Cultural Commonalities across Communities

Political:

"You start at your most popular and least capable. You end at your most capable and least popular. And it is a privilege."

—Tony Blair, former prime minister of Great Britain, on *Morning Joe*, 9-20-17

"Always remember others may hate you but those who hate you don't win unless you hate them. And then you destroy yourself."

—Richard M. Nixon, thirty-seventh US president, in his White House farewell address

Emergency Medicine:

"Women are still undervalued and earn less. Skilled professional women need to prove themselves to colleagues, superiors and subordinates (unlike male counterparts)."

—*Emergency Medicine News*, 5-8-17

Evolutionary Psychology:

You must act fast. There is a small window to act against abuse.

1) Psychological: dysfunction becomes new normal (drift, go along, adapt).
2) Resistance becomes more difficult with time, even dangerous. (Buss 1995)

Legal:

Motivation MICE: Money, Ideology, Coercion, Ego. (Crumpton 2012)

Entertainment:

"I am woman."

—Helen Reddy, 1971

Literary:

"Still I Rise."

—Maya Angelou, *The Complete Collected Poems of Maya Angelou*

Process and Communication for Action: The Bad and the Good

Suboptimal	Optimal
Problem	Opportunity to improve; issues exist; "Ever Better"
No structure	Structure; mutual understanding
No process	Process; collegial; not uneven power
No communication	Routine dialogue; rapport, understanding, respect
Negative feedback	Reassessment; problem solve together; teamwork
Different styles	Complementary styles
Emotion; nuisance	Thoughtful exploration; intelligent solutions for all stakeholders
Protracted process	Limited interaction required
Blame; negative narratives	TEAMSTEPPS; AHRQ

Effective Feedback

- Feedback is a dialogue to consider behavior change.
- Communication hopes to provide information about perceived work effectiveness. This will assist the person to achieve his or her goals.
- Feedback should be timely, specific (a behavior which an individual can address), descriptive, and nonjudgmental. A balanced description should include both positive and negative feedback. Feedback should be factual and without emotion.
- Both the perspectives and needs of the giver and receiver should be taken into account. Be respectful.
- Communication to ensure understanding avoids future discrepancies.
- Feedback should not be directed at the person himself or herself. Eliminate words that suggest bias.

Recognition of Errors to Find Opportunities

Information gaps, system flaws, low transparency, fear of failure

Cognitive biases—faulty skill set

Premature closure—stop assessment too early, before adequate information

Cognitive transfer to others

Anchoring—persistence of false idea despite new information

Confirmation bias—no feedback, no recalibration (need to welcome feedback)

Affective errors—based on negative emotions (influences decisions; less time, premature closure, remove individual from environment)

Correction of errors: reflection, feedback from additional individuals

Errors are an unavoidable part of the decision-making process. Inadequate information, biases, and resource limitations may lead to errors. These errors may be transferred to others. Opportunities to correct errors are feasible if objectivity is encouraged and additional information is sought from a diverse group of individuals.

Beyond Credible Alternative Facts—My Story

False Narrative	Character Trait
False Narrative	**Character Trait**
Problem	Problem solver, activist, visionary
Unwarranted attack	Nonviolent advocate
Noncollegial	Team builder
Sees only her perspective	Cassandra syndrome; advocate for others
Unhappy	Perfect fit for skill set
Seeks leadership, undermines	Declines several positions, desires functional unit
Power, control, money	Functionality, fairness
Lacks accountability	Speaks truth to power; integrity
No apology	Not handmaid

Misrepresentations

Counseling session	General discussion
Refuses work	Requests additional responsibilities with appropriate recognition (e.g., title and/or compensation)

Harassment Avoidance

- Different values, points of view, and abilities exist in the workforce.
- Everyone counts. Include diversity in all work processes. Be more inclusive.
- Ineffective communication leads to confusion, lack of teamwork, and low morale.
- Increase adaptability for solutions to problems.
- Increase viewpoints and have a larger pool of ideas.
- Inspire everyone's highest ability.
- Discrimination is an adverse decision based on age, gender, orientation, religion, class, or disability.
- Supervisory role—listen, counsel, options, document, disciplinary action
- Bad behavior—attempt to resolve yourself, address problem, ask to stop, speak with supervisor
- Forms of Harassment:
  - Unwelcome conduct, derogatory comments
  - Insinuations
  - Intimidation
  - Demeaning, fearful statements
  - Hostile work environment
  - Supervisor minimization, escalation—removal from position because it's the only reasonable solution

Goals:

- Inclusion—create an environment where members feels they contribute to their fullest potential
- Quality, safety, performance:
    - o Improve process, reduce error
    - o Address issues
    - o Address disrespectful, inappropriate behavior

Suggested Readings and References

Achor, Shawn. *The Happiness Advantage, the Seven Principles of Positive Psychology That Fuel Success and Performance at Work*. New York: Crown Business Books, 2010.

Alkayat, Zena. *Library of Luminaries: Frida Kahlo: An Illustrated Biography*. Abingdon, Oxfordshire: Taylor & Francis, 2016.

Arizona State University. "Angry Men Gain Influence, Angry Women Lose Influence, Study Shows." *Science Daily* (October 26, 2015), www.sciencedaily.com/releases/2015/10/151026172546.htm,

Atwood, Margaret. *The Handmaid's Tale*. Boston: Houghton Mifflin Company, 1986.

Badenhorst, W., and P. Hughes. "Psychological Aspects of Perinatal Loss." *Best Practice & Research in Clinical Obstetrics & Gynecology* 21 (2007): 249–259.

Banaji, Mahzarin R., Anthony G. Greenwald, and Eric Martin. *Blindspot: Hidden Biases of Good People*. New York: Delacorte Press, 2013.

Gender-Based Shifts in Content and Consistency of Judgment." *Social Psychological and Personality Science* 3, no. 2 (2012): 186–192.

Benner, Katie. "Women in Tech Speak Frankly on Culture of Harassment." *New York Times,* June 30, 2017, https://www.nytimes.com/2017/06/30/technology/women-entrepreneurs-speak-out-sexual-harassment.html.

Bennett, Jessica. *Feminist Fight Club: An Office Survival Manual for a Sexist Workplace.* New York: Harper Wave, 2016.

Biernat, Monica, M. J. Tocci, and Joan C. Williams. "The Language of Performance Evaluations.

Brown, Brene. *Daring Greatly: How the Courage to Be Vulnerable Transforms the Way We Live, Love, Parent, and Lead.* London. Penguin Publishing Group, 2012.

Brzezinski, Mika. *Knowing Your Value: Women, Money, and Getting What You're Worth.* New York: Weinstein Books, 2011.

Buss, David. "Evolutionary Psychology: A New Paradigm for Psychological Science." *Psychological Inquiry* 6, no. 1 (1995), 1–30.

Carlson, Gretchen. *Be Fierce: Stop Harassment and Take Your Power Back.* New York: Hachette Book Group, 2017.

Carnegie, Dale. *How to Win Friends and Influence People.* Simon and Schuster, 1936.

Carter, Nancy M., and Christina Silva. "The Myth of The Ideal Worker: Does Doing All the Right Things Really Get Women Ahead?" Catalyst (2011), http://www.catalyst.org/knowledge/myth-ideal-worker-does-doing-all-right-things-really-get-women-ahead.

Castilla, Emilio J., and Steven Benard. "The Paradox of Meritocracy in Organizations." *Administrative Science Quarterly* 55 (2010): 543–576. https://dspace.mit.edu/openaccess-disseminate/1721.1/65884.

Cauterucci, Christina. "The Majority of American Men Believe Sexism Is Over, According to a New Poll." *Slate* (August 18, 2016). www.slate.com/ ... /2016/08/18/the_majority_of_u_s_men_believe_sexism_is_over.ht

Chang, Emily. *Brotopia*. New York: Penguin Random House, 2018.

Choo, Esther. "Do Patients Fare Better Under Female Physicians?" *Emergency Physicians Monthly* (February 2017).

Christie, Agatha. *Murder on the Orient Express*. New York. Berkley Books, 1933.

Comstock, Beth. "How Diversity Fuels Innovation." Interview by Andrew Ross Sorkin, Vanity Fair New Establishment Summit, October 14, 2016 (video). https://video. Vanity Fair. Com/watch/the/New/Establishment-Summit-How/Diversity-Fuels-Innovation.

Contorno, Steve. "Rand Paul Says More Than Half of Students at Medical, Dental and Law Schools Are Females." *Politifact* (January 28, 2014). http://www.politifact,com/truth-o-meter/statements/2014/jan/28/rand-paul/Rand-Paul-says-More-Half-Students-Medical-Dental-a.

Cook-Garza, Kennedy. "The Cool Girl Trap: Or Why Sexism in Tech Isn't Going Away." *Medium* (October 6, 2015). https:medium.com/endless/the-cool-girl-trap-or-why-sexism-in-tech-isn-t-going-away-825b9a7642f5.

Correll, Shelley J. "Reducing gender biases in modern workplaces: A small wins approach to organizational change." (2017). *Gender & Society* 31(6): 725-750.

Covert, Bryce. "About a Third of Women Have Experienced Discrimination in the Workplace." *Think Progress* (August 19, 2013).

DeWolf, Mark. "12 Stats about Working Women." US Department of Labor Blog (March 1, 2017). https://blog.dol.gov/2017/03/01/12-stats-about-working-women.

Dickens, Charles. *A Tale of Two Cities*. London. Chapman and Hall, 1859.

Dobbin, Frank, and Alexandra Kalev. "Why Diversity Programs Fail." *Harvard Business Review* (July–August 2016). https://hbr.org/2016/07/why-diversity-programs-fail.

Eastman, P.D. *Are You My Mother?* New York: Random House, 1960.

Emba, Christine. "America Badly Needs Relationship Counseling." *The Washington Post*, July 5, 2017.

Engel, George L. "The Clinical Application of the Biopsychosocial Model." *The Journal of Medicine and Philosophy: A Forum for Bioethics and Philosophy of Medicine* 6, no. 2 (January 1, 1981): 101–124. https://academic.oup.com/jmp/article/6/2/101/896145.

Engel, George L. "The Death of a Twin: Mourning and Anniversary Reactions—Fragments of 10 Years of Self-analysis." *Int J Psychoanal* 56 (1976): 23–40.

Evans, Melanie. "Female Doctors' Hospital Patients May Have An Edge." *Wall Street Journal*, December 19, 2016.

Feeney, Nolan. "Women Are Now More Likely to Have College Degree Than Men." *Time* (October 7, 2015). http://time.com/4064665/women-College-degree.

Felton, O. "Diversity Matters: Gender Equality An Achievable Goal." *Emergency Medicine News*. Alphen aan den Rijn. Wolters Kluwer. (2017). *39* no. *5* (May 2017): 8. doi: 10.1097/01.EEM.0000516454.52864.96.

Flake, Jeff. *Conscience of a Conservative: A Rejection of Destructive Politics and a Return to Principle.* New York. Random House, 2017.

Forrest, G. C., E. Standish, and J. D. Baum. "Support after Perinatal Death: A Study of Support and Counselling after Perinatal Bereavement." *British Medical Journal* 285 (1982): 1475–1479.

Fouad, Nadya A. "Women's Reasons for Leaving the Engineering Field." *Frontiers in Psychology* (June 30, 2017). https://doi.org/10.3389/fpsyg.2017.00875.

Frankl, Viktor. *Man's Search for Meaning.* Boston: Beacon Press, 1946.

Free Library. "School Placement and Separation of Twins: A Review of Research." www.freepatentsonline.com/article/Childhood-Education/220467991.html.

Friedman, Thomas. *Thank You for Being Late: An Optimist's Guide to Thriving in the Age of Accelerations. New York.* Farrar, Straus and Giroux, 2016.

Fromme, K., W. R. Corbin, and M. I. Kruse. "Behavioral Risks During the Transition from High School to College." *Developmental Psychology* 44 no. 5 (2008): 1497–1504. 10.1037/a0012614.

Giang, Vivian. "The Growing Business of Detecting Unconscious Bias." *Fast Company* (May 5, 2015). https://www.fastcompany.com/3045899/the-growing-business-of-detecting-unconscious-bias.

Gillibrand, Kirsten. *Off the Sidelines: Speak up, Be Fearless, and Change Your World*. New York: Ballantine Books, 2014.

Goldin, Claudia, Lawrence F. Katz, and Ilyana Kuziemko. "The Homecoming of American College Women: The Reversal of the College Gender Gap." *Journal of Economic Perspectives* 20 no. 4 (2006): 133.

Gonzales, Laurence. *Deep Survival: Who Lives, Who Dies, and Why*. New York: W. W. Norton & Company, 2004.

Gray, Emma. "Amy Schumer's 'I'm Sorry' Skewers a Culture That Makes Women Apologize Constantly." *Huffington Post* (May 5, 2015). http://www.huffingtonpost.com/2015/05/14/amy-shcumer--im-sorry-not-sorry_n_7276504.html.

Halter, Jeffrey Tobias. *Why Women: The Leadership Imperative to Advancing Women and Engaging Men*. Roswell: Fushian, 2015.

"Harvard Business School Dean Apologizes to All Women." *Huffington Post*, January 31, 2014, http://www.huffingtonpost.com/2014/01/31/harvard-business-school-women_n_4697113.html.

Hegewisch, Ariane, Claudia Williams, and Anlan Zhang, "The Gender Wage Gap: 2011." Washington, DC: Institute for Women's Policy Research (March 2012), http://www.iwpr.org/publications/pubs/the-gender-wage-gap-2011.

Heron, Sheryl. "Looking Forward: How Emergency Departments Can Embrace Diversity and Inclusion." *ACEP Now.* Irving. December 2016.

Holmes, Anna. "Maybe You Should Read the Book: The Sheryl Sandberg Backlash." *The New Yorker,* March 4, 2013, <u>https://www.newyorker.com/books/page-turner/Maybe-you-should-read-the-book-the-Sheryl-sandberg/backlash</u>.

Huffington, Arianna. *Thrive: The Third Metric to Redefining Success and Creating a Life of Well-Being, Wisdom, and Wonder.* New York: Harmony Books, 2014.

Inesi, Ena. "It's All about Control." *Psychological Science.* London: Association for Psychological Science (2011).

Johnson, W. Brad. *"On Being a Mentor: A Guide for Higher Education Faculty"* second edition. Mahwah: Lawrence Erlbaum Associates, 2015. https://books.google.com.

Johnson, W. Brad; and David Smith. *Athena Rising: How and Why Men Should Mentor Women.* London: Routledge, 2016.

Jordan, Hillary. *Mudbound.* New York. <u>Workman Publishing Company</u>, 2008.

Kantor, Jodi. "A Brand New World in Which Men Ruled." *The New York Times,* December 23, 2014.

Kass, Dara. "'Amplification' Helps Lessen Bias against Women." *Emergency Medicine News.* Philadelphia: Lippincott Williams & Wilkins (March 2017).

Kay, Katty, and Claire Shipman. *The Confidence Code: The Science and Art of Self-Assurance—What Women Should Know.* New York: Harper Business, 2014.

Koenig, A. M. (1), A. H. Eagly, A. A. Mitchell, and T. Ristikari. "Are Leader Stereotypes Masculine? A Meta-analysis of Three Research Paradigms." *Psychol Bull.* 137 no. 4 (July 2011): 616–642. doi: 10.1037/a0023557.

Krzanich, Brian. (August 16, 2017). money.cnn.com/2017/08/16/news/ceo-quotes-charlottesville-trump/index.html)

Lam, Jackie. "The EMN Salary Survey." *Emergency Medicine News.* Philadelphia: Lippincott Williams & Wilkins (June 2018).

Lang, Ilene H. "Catalyst Study Reveals Financial Performance Is Higher for Companies with More Women at the Top," Catalyst (January 15, 2004). http://www.catalyst.org/media/catalyst-study-reveals-financial-performance-higher-companies-more-women-top.

Lautenberger, Diana, Valerie M. Dandar, Claudia L. Raezer, and Rae Anne Sloan. "The State of Women in Academic Medicine: The Pipeline and Pathways to Leadership." Washington, DC: Association of American Medical Colleges (2014). https://members.aamc.org/eweb/upload/The%20State%20of%20Women%20in%20Academic%20Medicine%202013-2014%20FINAL.pdf.

Lee, Harper. *To Kill a Mockingbird.* Philadelphia. J. B. Lippincott & Co, 1960.

Lewis, Rebecca J. "Beyond Dominance: The Importance of Leverage." *The Quarterly Review of Biology* 77, no. 2 (June 2002), 149–164. DOI: 10.1086/343899. https://www.jstor.org/stable/10.1086/343899.

Lindberg, Sara M., Janet Shibley Hyde, and Jennifer L. Peterson. "New Trends in Gender and Mathematics Performance: A Meta-analysis." *Psychological Bulletin* 136 no. 6 (2010): 1123–1135. https://doi.org:10.1037/a0021276.

Lipman, Joanne. *That's What She Said*. New York: Harper Collins, 2018.

Lublin, Joann S. "Bringing Hidden Biases into the Light." *Wall Street Journal,* January 9, 2014, https://www.wsj.com/articles/bringing-hidden-biases-into-the-light-1389311814.

Marcotte, Amanda. "New Research Shows That Men Feel Insecure When Their Partners Succeed, but Women Don't." Slate, August 30, 2013, http://www.slate.com/blogs/xx_ factor/2013/08/30/gender_differences_and_self_esteem_new_research_shows_that_men_feel_Insecure.html.

Martin, Sean R. "Research: Men Get Credit for Voicing Ideas, but Not Problems. Women Don't Get Credit for Either." Harvard Business Review (November 2, 2017).

Mass, Wendy. *The Candymakers*. New York: Little Brown, 2010

Maxwell, John: *How Successful People Lead*. Lake Arrowhead: Hawking Books, 2010.

McCarthy, Andrew. "Trump Has Himself, Not Sessions, to Blame for the Limitless Mueller Investigation." *National Review,* July 22, 2017, https://www.nationalreview.com/2017/07/donald-trump-jeff-sessions-president-blame-mueller-affair.

McDaniel, S. H., D. S. Morse, S. Reis, E. A. Edwardsen, M. G. Gurnsey, A. Taupin, J. J. Griggs, and C. G. Shields. "Physicians Criticizing Physicians to Patients." *JGIM* 28 no. 11 (2013): 1405–1409.

McGinn, Kathleen L., and Nicole Tempest. "Heidi Roizen." Harvard Business School Case 800-228, January 2000 (revised April 2010.)

Mei, Jenny. "Research Links Sugar Consumption, Fat Production, and Diabetes." *Yale Scientific* (April 3, 2011). www.yalescientific.org/ ... /research-links-sugar-consumption-fat-production-and-diabetes.

Miller, Claire Cain: "The Motherhood Penalty vs. the Fatherhood Bonus," New York Times, Sept. 6, 2014, https://www.nytimes.com/2014/09/07/upshot/a-child-helps-your-career-if-youre-a-man.html.

Montella, Erin Callan. *Full Circle: A Memoir of Leaning in Too Far and the Journey Back.* Sanibel, FL. Triple M Press, 2016.

Morgan, James. "Women 'Better at Multitasking' Than Men, Study Finds." BBC (October 24, 2013). http://www.bbc.com/news/science-environment-24645100.

Orman, Suze. *Women & Money: Owning the Power to Control Your Destiny.* New York: Spiegel & Grau, 2007.

Orwell, George. *Nineteen Eighty-four.* London: Secker & Warburg, 1949.

Pao, Ellen: *Reset: My Fight for Inclusion and Lasting Change.* New York: Random House, 2017.

Parker, Ceri. "'When the Woman Starts Talking the Men Switch Off'— Christine Lagarde on Why Gender Parity Is Taking so Long." World Economic Forum (January 18, 2017). https://www.weforum.org/agenda/2017/01/when- the-woman-starts-talking-the-men-switch-off-davos-participants-on-why-gender-parity-is-taking-so-long.

Plank, Kevin. (August 14, 2017). https://www.forbes.com/ ... /kevi n-plank-follows-ken-frazier-and-quits-president-trump).

Pollack, William S. "Retirement Is Your Reward for a Long Work Life, but Research Suggests That Continuing to Work in Some Way May Offer a Big Payday for Your Health." Boston: Harvard Health Publishing (March 2016). https://www.health.harvard.edu/ staying-healthy/retired-men-at-work.

Prime, Jeanine, and Corinne A. Moss-Racusin. "Engaging Men in Gender Initiatives: What Change Agents Need to Know." Catalyst (May 4, 2009). http://www.Catalyst.org/knowledge/engaging-me n-gender-initiatives-what-change-agents need-know.

Quart, Alyssa. *Squeezed: Why Our Families Can't Afford America.* New York: Harper Collins, 2018.

Reuben, E., Paola Sapienza, and Luigi Zingales. "How Stereotypes Impair Women's Careers in Science." *PNAS* 111 no. 12 (March 25, 2014): 4403–4408. https://www.ncbi.nlm.nih.gov/pmc/articles/ PMC3970474.

Richards, Cecile. *Make Trouble: Standing Up, Speaking Out, and Finding the Courage to Lead—My Life Story.* New York: Simon and Schuster, 2018.

Rivera, Lauren A. "Guess Who Doesn't Fit in at Work." *New York Times* (May 30, 2015). https://www.nytimes.com/2015/05/31/opinion/ sunday/guess-who-doesnt-fit-in-at-work.html?_r=o.

Robbins, Anthony J. "I Promise You ... Your Competition Isn't Beating You Because They Are Working More Hours Than You. It's Because They Are Working Smarter." Twitter post (May 29, 2017). https:// Twitter.com/blakeir/status/86927512971243393.

Rudman, Laurie A. "Self-promotion as a Risk Factor for Women: The Costs and Benefits of Counter Stereotypical Impression Management." *Journal of Personality and Social Psychology* 74 no. 3 (1998): 629–645. https://dokumen.tips›Documents.

Ruiz, Rebecca. "What To Do When You're a Woman and a Man Takes Credit for Your Success." Mashable (February 17, 2016). http://mashable.com/2016/02/17/man-takes-credit-woman/#5wprmWjaNmqK.

Samsel, Michael. "Grooming." Abuse and Relationships. 2008. www.abuseandrelationships.org/ ... /grooming ...

Sandberg, Sheryl. *Lean In: Women, Work, and the Will to Lead*. New York: Alfred A. Knopf, 2013.

Sandberg, Sheryl. "Sheryl Sandberg: Women Are Leaning In—But They Face Pushback." *Wall Street Journal* (September 27, 2016). https://www.wsj.com/articles/sheryl-sandberg-women-are-leaning-inbut-they-face-pushback-1474963980.

Sandberg, Sheryl. Facebook post on ending sexual harassment. Menlo Park. December 4, 2017. https://work.qz.com/1145659/read-sheryl-sandbergs-facebook-post-on-sexual-harassment-and-sexism-at-work/

Silverman, Michael. "Praise and Polish: The Fine Art of Good Feedback." Emergency Physicians Monthly (May 2017).

Silverman, Michael. "Your Staff Meetings Are Broken. Here's How to Fix Them." Emergency Physicians Monthly (February 2017).

Simons, Daniel J., and Christopher Chabris. "Invisible Gorilla." Boston: Harvard University, 1999.

Simons, S. S., and E. R. Goddess. "Enough!" *Emergency Medicine News.* Philadelphia: Lippincott Williams & Wilkins, 2017.

Sinclair, Upton. *The Jungle.* New York. Doubleday, Jabber & Company, 1906.

Smith, Lindsay, Ruth Webber, and John DeFrain. "Spiritual Well-Being and Its Relationship to Resilience in Young People: A Mixed Methods Case Study." *Sage Open Journal* 3 no. 2 (April 29, 2013). https://doi.org/10.1177/2158244013485582.

Snyder, Kieran. "The Abrasiveness Trap: High-Achieving Men and Women Are Described Differently in Reviews." Fortune (August 26, 2014). http://fortune.com/2014/08/26/performance-review-gender-bias.

Solnit, Rebecca. *Men Explain Things to Me.* Chicago: Haymarket Books, 2014.

Strauss, Valerie. "A Disturbing Truth about Medical School—And America's Future Doctors." *Washington Post,* May 8, 2017.

Streitfeld, David. "In Ellen Pao's Suit vs Kleiner Perkins, World of Venture Capital Is under Microscope." *New York Times* (March 5, 2015). https://www.nytimes.com/2015/ ... /in-ellen-paos-suit-vs-kleiner-perkins-world-of-vent.

Swim, Janet K., and Lawrence J. Sanna. "He's Skilled, She's Lucky: A Meta-Analysis of Observers' Attributions for Women's and Men's Successes and Failures." *Personality and Social Psychology Bulletin* (May 1, 1996). journals.sagepub.com/doi/abs/10.1177/0146167296225008.

Thomas, David A., and Robin J. Ely. "Making Differences Matter: A New Paradigm for Managing Diversity." *Harvard Business Review* (September–October 1996).

Thompson, Jeff. (2012). "Beyond Words. The Science of Body Language & the Debates. Research Shows That Yes, Body Language Does Matter." *Psychology Today* (October 21, 2012).

Tobar, Hector. "Neckbeard, Mansplain. Now in Oxford Dictionaries Online: Amazeballs." *LA Times* (August 14, 2014). http://www.latimes. com/books/jacketcopy/la-et-jc-neckbeard-mansplain-amazeballs-oxford-dictionary-words-20140814-story.html.

Turner, Caroline. *Difference Works: Improving Retention, Productivity and Profitability through Inclusion.* California: Live Oak Press LLC, 2012.

Uhlmann, Eric, and Geoffrey L. Cohen. "Constructed Criteria: Redefining Merit to Justify Discrimination." *American Psychological Society* 16 no. 6 (2005). journals.sagepub.com/doi/abs/10.1111/j.0956-7976.2005.01559.x.

Verel, Patrick. "Being the Breadwinner Still Large Part of Male Identity, Study Finds." Fordham I University (August 23, 2012). https://news.fordham.edu › Inside Fordham.

Wieczner, Jen. "Hillary Clinton Is the First to Say 'I'm Sorry' in a Presidential Concession Speech." *Fortune* (November 14, 2016). http://fortune.com/2016/11/14/hilary-clinton-concession-speech-sorry-hallelujah/

Wiens, Kandi, and Annie McKee. "Why Some People Get Burned Out and Others Don't." Boston: *Harvard Business Review* (November 23, 2016).

Wiley, Mary Glenn, and Arlene Eskilson. "The Interaction of Sex and Power Base on Perceptions of Managerial Effectiveness." *Academy of Management*. Published online November 30, 2017. https://journals. aom.org/toc/amj/25/3.

Williams, Joan C. and Kate Massinger, "How Women Are Harassed Out of Science," *The Atlantic*, July 25, 2016.

Williams, Melissa J. "The Price Women Leaders Pay for Assertiveness— And How to Minimize It." *Wall Street Journal* (May 31, 2016). https://www.wsj.com/articles/the-price-women-leaders-pay-for-assertiveness-and-how-to-minimize -it-1464660240.

Wolff, Michael. *Fire and Fury*. New York. Little Brown, 2018.

Women's Media Center. "The Problem." January 1, 2012. http://www. womensmediacenter.com/pages/the-problem.

Zarya, Valentina. "What Women Want from Their Employers, in 5 Simple Charts." *Fortune* (January 19, 2016). http://fortune. com/2016/01/20/what- women-want-charts.

Women's Empowerment
and Rights Resources

- Abuse and Relationships (abuseandrelationships.org)
- The American Association of University Women (aauw.org)
- Domestic Abuse Intervention Programs. 202 East Superior Street. Duluth, MN 66802
  218-722-2781
- Institute for Women's Leadership (womensleadership.com)
- Lean In (leanin.org)
- Workplace Fairness (workplacefairness.org)

Acknowledgments for Messengers of Hope

My parents: a mother who always told me my best was good enough, and a father who believed a daughter could be a physician in his footsteps.

My children: a son who will continue the journey for equality in medicine, and two daughters who share my desire for equality and tolerance in the world.

My husband, who supported me through the difficult times and shared my values.

Faith leaders: You are loved. You are not alone.

Friends, roommates, housemates, and classmates: You have a friend.

Primary and secondary teachers: You can dream.

College professors: You can lead change.

University role models, supportive female chairwomen, emergency observation unit team: You can do it.

Medical caregivers: You are resilient.

Advocacy groups: You are not to blame.

About the Author

Pandora B. Angel, MD, completed her medical degree in 1986 and a residency in internal medicine in 1989. She was a practicing physician for thirty years, twenty-three of those as an emergency physician at a university medical center and an affiliated hospital. At the time of her retirement in 2017, she was an associate professor of emergency medicine. During her tenure, Angel spearheaded clinical initiatives to improve efficiency and quality care for all emergency patients.

Printed and bound by PG in the USA